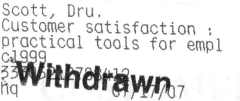

R SATISFACTION

Practical Tools for Employees of Santa Clara County

Dru Scott, Ph.D

CREDITS

Editors: **Ilene Shapera and Debbie Woodbury**
Production Manager: **Judy Petry**
Text and Layout Design: **Amy Shayne**
Production Artists: **Robin Strobel, Kay Green**
Cover Design: **County of Santa Clara**

www.crisplearning.com

99 00 01 02   10 9 8 7 6 5 4 3 2 1

Library of Congress Catalog Card Number 88-70488
Scott, Dru
Customer Satisfaction: Practical Tools for
Building Important Relationships
ISBN 1-56052-523-1

This book is printed
on recyclable paper
with soy ink.

PRINTED WITH
SOY INK

County of Santa Clara
Employee Services Agency

County Government Center, East Wing
70 West Hedding Street, 8th Floor
San Jose, California 95110
(408) 299-4355 FAX 295-3012

This book is dedicated to the Employees of Santa Clara County.

Quality public service is at the forefront of the mission of the County of Santa Clara. Service, in fact, is the reason we exist. We do not manufacture a product. Rather, we provide a variety of services, from law and justice to health and social services to environmental services, and a myriad of others. We are often called upon to serve people under personal and financial stress and crisis, people from diverse backgrounds, often unacquainted with the process or workings of government.

It is for these reasons that you, as employees of Santa Clara County, need a variety of "tools" to do your jobs effectively, efficiently, and compassionately. This book, and the training that accompanies it, is one of those tools.

The Department of Equal Opportunity and Employee Development is committed to furthering the vision of our diverse organization by promoting learning and respect within our organization and to the customers we serve, both internal and external. As a part of our ongoing effort to enable employees to develop their professional skills and to instill a philosophy of lifelong learning, we are proud to dedicate this book, *Customer Satisfaction—Practical Tools for Employees of Santa Clara County* to you, the employees of Santa Clara County. We hope you will use it as a tool to enable you to better serve our customers.

Maria R. Dupras

Maria R. Dupras
Director, Department of Equal Opportunity and Employee Development

Board of Supervisors: Donald F. Gage, Bianca Alvarado, Pete McHugh, James T. Beall Jr., S. Joseph Simitian
County Executive: Richard Wittenberg

9-007

The Mission of the Department of Equal Opportunity and Employee Development is:

To Further the Vision of Our Diverse Organization By Promoting Learning and Respect

In order to achieve the mission of the County to provide quality public services to a changing and diverse community, the Employee Development Division will facilitate, in a positive and supportive manner, the process of professional and personal growth of employees. They will accomplish this by:

★ Maintaining a knowledgeable, healthy, skilled, and culturally competent workforce;

★ Providing a safe and respectful work environment;

★ Fostering empowerment and accountability at all levels;

★ Developing and supporting the leadership skills of employees;

★ Aligning training programs with organizational values and goals;

★ Ensuring high quality training through coordinated resources, appropriate technology, effective partnerships, and ongoing measurement.

All Employee Development programs are designed to support this mission and goals.

Learning Objectives For:

CUSTOMER SATISFACTION

Practical Tools for Employees of Santa Clara County

The objectives of this book are to:

- ❑ explain why satisfying customers, the people part of your job, is as important as doing the technical part of your job

- ❑ show how to use the tools of customer satisfaction

- ❑ provide techniques of overcoming barriers to customer satisfaction

Assessing Your Progress

A twenty-five item multiple choice/true-false review is presented, along with the listed objectives each question covers. When you complete and submit the response sheet located at the end of this book, you will receive a Certificate of Completion for the coursework. If you have any questions, call us at Employee Development: 408-299-2186.

Copy, cut out, and post these helpful reminders.

"Good customer relationship skills save me time, help every area of my life and are well worth learning."

"This is my job, and I like it. Not because it is easy. Not because there are no difficult people. Not because there are no frustrations. People are a part of any job. So I make things easier for myself by taking things professionally."

"Even though burnout is common, it is not mandatory. I take care of myself so that I keep myself up, energetic and thinking clearly."

"Even if it is not easy, I treat each person during my workday as a customer. It always pays off. I get better cooperation. And I get the satisfaction of working as a partner."

"Because I do not want to waste my time, I ask questions and listen to learn exactly what others expect from me. They appreciate it, and it makes my job easier."

"I solve problems without blaming myself or others. It saves everyone time. It reduces stress, and it builds teamwork."

"I make it easy for people to cooperate with me. I find good techniques which can be tailored to fit my personality and the situation. I have less frustration because I use the techniques at every opportunity."

"I go out of my way to get feedback from my customers. It makes my job easier, and it keeps me going strong."

"Using good customer relationship skills saves me time, helps my professional and personal life and adds to my long-term success."

Contents

Sneak Preview: The Big Picture x
Personal Customer Satisfaction Action Plan xi

PART I: CLEARING THE BARRIERS

Chapter 1. How Customer Relationship Skills Can Build Your Success
Building Customer Relationships for Repeat Business 4
Success Stories 6

Chapter 2. Dealing with Difficult People
Job Frustrations and Difficult People 12
The Secret of Success 15
Save Time by Taking Situations Professionally 18
Keep the Spotlight on the Issue 19

Chapter 3. Burnout–Threat to Customer Satisfaction
Eight Common Signs of Burnout 22
Additional Signs of Burnout 24
Five Techniques for Preventing Burnout 26

Chapter 4. The Secret to Getting More Cooperation
Updating Your Beliefs 36
A Selfish and Successful Strategy for Getting More Cooperation 37
Roadblocks to Avoid 38
Working as Partners–Treating Your Boss as a Customer 41

PART II: BUILDING THE FOUNDATION

Chapter 5. The Problem with Customer Service
Satisfaction is Defined by the Customer 48
Meet the Requirements of the People You Serve 49
Customer Satisfaction Is Easier When You Have Targets 50
A Shortcut for Defining Targets 53
The Pleasant Payoff 55

Chapter 6. The Customer Is Not Always Right, But...
The Customer is Always the Customer 58
Blaming–A Barrier to Problem Solving 59
Shortcut to Stopping the Blame Habit 61
Seven Practical Steps to Customer Problem Solving 62

Contents (CONTINUED)

PART III: USING THE TOOLS

Chapter 7. Getting What You Want

Make It Easy for Others to Cooperate with You 78

Six Cooperation Techniques 79

Chapter 8. Building Motivation with Customer Feedback

People Need to Know How They Are Doing 96

A Simple System for Obtaining Feedback 100

Protect Yourself with Ongoing Feedback 101

Get Systematic Feedback from Your Customers 102

The Best Kind of Customer Feedback 103

Talk About Customer Feedback 105

Chapter 9. How to Keep It Going

Success Secret 1: Give Yourself More Blue Ribbons .108

Success Secret 2: Hand Out More Blue Ribbons 109

Success Secret 3: Treat This Book As a Tool Kit 110

Remember the Customer Satisfaction Essentials 113

Your Feedback Is Important 115

Author's Suggested Responses 116

About the Author

Author, film personality, psychologist and seminar speaker, Dru Scott is an internationally known authority on customer satisfaction. Dru has been featured in six films and has authored six books with combined sales of over one million copies. Her client list includes such organizations as DuPont, AT&T, American Express, the American Dental Association and the University of California, among many others.

Sneak Preview: The Big Picture

CHAPTER 1

Customer satisfaction skills with build your success because you can use these relationship skills to succeed inside and outside the organization.

CHAPTER 2

Get a head start on dealing with difficult people by taking it professionally and not personally.

CHAPTER 3

Since burnout is a major threat to customer satisfaction, spot the eight signals of it and prevent it five ways.

CHAPTER 4

The secret of getting more cooperation is to treat each persona as a customer whether inside or outside the organization.

CHAPTER 5

The problem with customer service is that it is defined by the provider. The reward of customer satisfaction grows because it is defined by the customer. Consequently, aim for satisfaction.

CHAPTER 6

Even though the customer is not always right, the customer is always the customer, so solve the problems without blaming.

CHAPTER 7

The secret to getting what you want is to save time with proven techniques including four fast and friendly language shortcuts.

CHAPTER 8

Build team motivation with systematic and on-going customer feedback.

CHAPTER 9

Keep your individual motivation going with the fun of finding new ways to reinforce yourself.

Personal Customer Satisfaction Action Plan

You will be working with more than 50 practical, proven techniques in this book. View them as you would a buffet. Pick the ones that are most beneficial for your work responsibilities, your pressures, your priorities and the people in your life.

Concentrate on up to five techniques. Selecting more will encourage you to put them aside. Even if you only pick three or four, that is fine. When you pick the right ones for you and concentrate on putting them to work, you reap rich rewards. You reinforce habits that reduce your stress and build job satisfaction.

Fold the corner of this page because it is a useful place to which to return as you work through the book. When you discover a technique that would be especially well-suited to your responsibilities, write it in the space provided below. Then use the list of techniques that you select to help you tackle any troublesome areas.

YOUR PERSONAL SATISFACTION ACTION PLAN

What customer satisfaction techniques would benefit you if you used them more frequently?

Page
Reference

1. _____   _____

2. _____   _____

3. _____   _____

4. _____   _____

5. _____   _____

PART

1

CLEARING THE BARRIERS

How Customer Relationship Skills Can Build Your Success

Use These Skills Inside and Outside Your Organization, Today and Tomorrow

PREVIEW

Even though it is easier to be successful when you use good customer relationship skills, few people have been taught these skills.

Here is the bonus. Customer relationship skills add to every area of your life because they are really relationship skills. You can use these skills with external customers and with people inside your organization. You can also use them with your family and friends.

The reward for using these skills effectively is the opportunity for repeat business and long-term, mutually satisfying relationships.

As you turn to the next page, you may be asking, "This sounds good, but how do you know the ideas actually work?"

❖

Building Customer Relationships for Repeat Business

The author shares the story behind the approach.

"When I sat at a table in the coffee shop at San Francisco International Airport and watched an executive from DuPont take a leather calendar from inside his suit jacket, slide out a gold Cross pen and start to turn the pages, I had no idea how this would change my work and my life.

The call

"As I watched him, I thought about his phone call three weeks ago asking about an article I had written on customer satisfaction. The article shared the research behind two of my films that had just been released. It told how decision makers can help everyone in the organization stay focused on customers. During that phone call, he had asked more questions and then wanted to know when we could talk face to face.

The turning point

"Our talk during his stopover at San Francisco International Airport was the start of my getting on planes every month to consult with and lead seminars for a range of DuPont groups and customers in Wilmington, Delaware, at plant sites across the U.S. and in Europe. In the period that followed, I helped multiply valuable lessons from DuPont's long-term successes. That 12-year period changed me and what I do in several ways.

"It was during that time I was challenged to research and measure the results of our seminars. During that time of researching and validating what brought about sustained improvements in performance, my approach shifted drastically. That shift has been confirmed in my work with dozens of other organizations over the years and it has generated results three ways."

Shift Your Focus

Shift your focus and enjoy more long-term success three ways:

1. Rather than only seeing customers, focus on satisfying customers—you will feel better.

2. Rather than only filling requests, focus on filling requests in ways that build your relationships—you will have more satisfaction.

3. Rather than only thinking about the needs of today, keep your eye on earning the opportunity for repeat business tomorrow—you will enjoy more rewards.

The secret

For more long-term success, build such good customer relationships that people turn to you with their repeat business.

Success Stories

"Building Customer Relationship for Repeat Business" is more than a motto on the wall. It is a way of relating that helps every area of your life, today and tomorrow.

As you read the following inspirational stories, you will see how different people used the various tools presented throughout this book to help in some area of their lives.

The purpose of the stories is to encourage you to read each chapter and find the tools that will help you in some area of your life.

Success Stories

SUCCESS STORY 1
Ann Puts Up a Sign

When Ann drove her car into the parking lot at work, she was still tired. She had been up until midnight arguing with her oldest son. She had never planned to be the single parent of two teenage boys, and she had never planned to hear what they dumped on her. They told her they did not like her rules, her cooking, her nagging or their house.

She had worked so hard to take care of them since her husband had died that she had hoped they would appreciate some of her sacrifices. But they did not. At least not now.

So Ann decided to take home a small sign she made from the chapter on dealing with difficult people. She taped these words to her bathroom mirror: "Take it professionally, not personally."

Later she told a friend at lunch, "It's still not easy, but I picture that small sign on my mirror, and it helps me have a little more objectivity and strength."

SUCCESS STORY 2
Bill Suspects Burnout

It did not happen all at once; however, Bill suspected something was wrong. He had started getting into work late, not saying anything in meetings, getting less done and feeling fatigued even when he crawled out of the covers in the morning. At breakfast, he had even avoided talking to his wife and started reading the cereal box.

Bill knew something was wrong when he read the eight warning signs in the chapter on burnout. He could check "yes" to five of the signs. He had let himself slide into burnout. He had blamed his job, but he began to see the situation from a different perspective.

He told himself that other people in the same job were not feeling burnout, so it probably was not the job that was causing his feelings. Then Bill made a promise to himself to put a "#1" on his monthly calendar every time he used the number-one way of getting out of burnout, which is described in Chapter 3.

SUCCESS STORY 3
Blair Frames Her Boss

As Blair stood by the coffee machine, she complained to a friend that her boss did not appreciate all she did. When her friend laughed at her naiveté, she was taken aback. Then hurt. Then irritated. And finally thoughtful.

After she thought about it overnight, she realized that what she had been doing was not working. So she decided to experiment with an idea she had read in the chapter on getting more cooperation. As much as she did not actually believe it, she decided to act as if her boss were her customer.

Two weeks later she explained to another friend, "This tip gives me a new frame to put around my boss's face." Then Blair smiled and added, "You know, this is going to help me with my boss, because I do know how to treat customers."

SUCCESS STORY 4
Jeff Breaks a Record

When Jeff saw the call identification flash on his phone, his first impulse was to not pick it up and to let the call go into voice mail. He knew this customer would complain about something. Last Friday, when this customer had called, Jeff had clicked on the timer, resigned himself and listened to the harangue for twelve minutes.

After the call on Friday, Jeff reminded himself that he did not give up when he was behind in a basketball game and he was not going to give up with this customer either. He prided himself on turning around irate customers in record time. That was one reason he had been asked to fill in for the head of the call center. So later that Friday afternoon, he opened his book to the chapter "The Customer Is Not Always Right, But..." to the pages on calming language and practiced the quick ways to calm people.

Now as he saw the call identification flash on his phone, he had a new game plan. Before the call could switch onto voice mail, Jeff took a deep breath and reached for the phone. The first time the customer paused for a breath, Jeff answered with calming language. There was a surprised hesitation before the customer could continue

Success Stories (CONTINUED)

with the harangue. The second time the customer paused for another breath, Jeff answered with yet another example of calming language. This time the hesitation lasted longer. Then the response changed to, "Well, I guess I don't need to say any more. You understand."

Jeff had barely finished following up on the request and hanging up the phone when he stood up, gave his neighbor a high five and called across the cubical, "It's a record. Turned that guy around in only four minutes!"

You will discover more details about these stories as you read the following chapters, but the most important stories are the ones you write.

WRITING YOUR OWN SUCCESS STORIES

Spotlight a situation. Use the tools that fit you. Enjoy the results.

1. **What is a situation with an external customer (or customer group) that you want to improve? Write a few words after "A" to clarify your thinking and the solution you are seeking. (Later, as you read the book, have fun coming back and adding parts B and C.)**

    A. *The situation:*

    B. *The tools you found and the action you took:*

    C. *The results:*

2. **What is a situation with someone in your organization that you want to improve?**

    A. *The situation:*

    B. *The tools you found and the action you took:*

    C. *The results:*

3. **Now, let's look at your personal life. What situation in that arena is ready for improvement?**

    A. *The situation:*

    B. *The tools you found and the action you took:*

    C. *The results:*

CHAPTER 1

── RECAP OF TECHNIQUES ──

To take away the most from this chapter, look at the following key concepts and check the ones that fit you.

❑ The relationship skills that help me with the people outside the organization also help me with the people I serve inside the organization.

❑ The same customer satisfaction skills even help with my relationships with my family and friends.

❑ The reward for using these skills effectively is twofold: More opportunities for repeat business and more relationships that are mutually satisfying and long-term.

For Reinforcement Say to Yourself:

"Good customer relationship skills save me time, help every area of my life and are well worth learning."

❖

It is easy to have good relationships with some people, but what about the difficult people? In the next chapter, you will find the number-one skill for handling difficult people.

CHAPTER 2

Dealing with Difficult People

Take It Professionally, Not Personally

P R E V I E W

No matter what organization you are part of, or what job you have, sooner or later, you will run into difficult people.

The toughest people with whom to deal are often not "outsiders" but within your organization.

The best way to work with difficult people is to approach them professionally and not personally.

Being professional means keeping the spotlight on the issue under discussion and away from yourself.

❖

Job Frustrations and Difficult People

"This job would be great if it weren't for the difficult people."

If you have echoed the words above at one time or another, you are not alone. The people part of a job is the biggest source of frustration for most people. "People" complications surface in a variety of ways.

Seven Frequent Frustrations

Consider your situation. Decide how each of the following seven frustrations relates to your present job. Put an "X" on the line to show the level of frequency of the problem in your normal job responsibilities.

1. **Others blame you for problems over which you have no control.**

    Does not happen   *Happens frequently*

2. **People pressure you with last-minute requests.**

    Does not happen   *Happens frequently*

3. **People who do not understand your job make decisions that directly affect your work.**

    Does not happen   *Happens frequently*

4. **People do not give you the right information or materials that you need to do your job.**

    Does not happen   *Happens frequently*

5. **People inside the organization do not cooperate with you when you want to serve outside customers.**

    Does not happen   *Happens frequently*

6. **People change their expectations once a job is underway.**

    Does not happen   *Happens frequently*

7. **People on whom you depend do not do their jobs correctly.**

    Does not happen   *Happens frequently*

Chances are you had at least one "X" in the far right of the line. If so, you are like a majority of your colleagues. This book will help you understand these common frustrations and help you deal with them. The next few pages will explore major job frustrations in more detail.

CHECK FOR FRUSTRATIONS AND CHALLENGES

As you read the following situations, see if you can identify the frustrations and challenges each individual is facing. Place a "✓" in the box for those that are common for you or someone in your organization.

Situation 1

I get frustrated about getting blamed for things I don't control. Others talk to me as though I caused the problem. When I tell them there is nothing I can do, they don't understand. They just get mad. But, there is nothing I can do. I can't lie about it.

❑ This feels or sounds familiar.

Situation 2

There is no cooperation around here. No wonder we can't meet our due dates. It's people inside our organization who are the problem. They are either late or give me the wrong information. They don't answer their phones. I have to call five times to get an answer, and then it is usually wrong. If the people inside the organization ever get their act together, it would be no problem for me to get my job done.

❑ This feels or sounds familiar.

Job Frustrations and Difficult People (CONTINUED)

Situation 3

The trouble with my job is that people who don't understand what I do are responsible for telling me what to do. This happens not just with our customers but also with people at the top of our organization. They don't understand how tough it is. Sometimes they don't even know enough to ask for what they want.

❑   This feels or sounds familiar.

If you have been working for more than a few months, you probably can name specific examples that sound like the situations presented above.

Every day, thousands of people in organizations like yours wrestle with these and similar frustrations. The situations described on the preceding page are tough. They are often unfair. And yet they are very common. If you encounter any of the seven frustrations listed on page 12, you would probably agree that the people part of the job is the part many employees would like to leave behind.

You are not alone when it comes to people-related problems. Even highly trained scientists need to get budgets approved and research accepted by others. Specialized craftspeople need others to obtain the necessary materials and market their products. Computer specialists find their technical abilities are not enough unless they can deal effectively with people. Analysts face the challenge of communicating complex information to lay people. No one is immune.

Each of us face frustrations and challenges whenever we interact on a regular basis with those ever so complicated creatures called people. Although it may often seem so, we probably realize the grass is not greener in another job. Finding improvement in a new organization or job rarely happens. Blaming your present job bears little fruit. The reality is clear. No matter what organization or job you are in, you eventually will run into difficult people, and you might as well develop your skill in dealing with them. The next several pages will assist you.

The Secret of Success

Take It Professionally, Not Personally

The secret to resolving most "people problems" is simple but not easy. It is like being told to "love your neighbor," which is often easier to say than to do. Nonetheless, when you learn to separate personal feelings from professional ones, the rewards are high. This book will teach you how to put this proven secret to work when you encounter difficult people.

Can you think of a situation where you took things personally and not professionally? Perhaps you lost your composure and said things you regretted later. Maybe you felt hurt and mistreated and let your concentration slip. Or you may have become defensive. If any of these sound familiar, take heart; it simply proves you are human.

A Personal Case

Think about a situation where you took things personally and then describe it in the space provided below.

The people? _____

_____

What was said? _____

_____

What was the setting? _____

_____

What was the timing? _____

_____

Other factors? _____

_____

The Secret of Success (CONTINUED)

Review the personal situation that you described on the previous page. Then determine the possible costs for taking the situation personally. Check any of the following items that apply.

BY TAKING THINGS PERSONALLY, I FELT:

❑ guilty

❑ like my concentration was interrupted

❑ like it hurt a relationship

❑ as though it dampened teamwork

❑ other _____

Taking things personally can hurt both you and others. Taking a situation professionally pays off for everyone.

To help avoid costly personal situations, learn to listen to yourself. By practicing, you can learn to recognize when you might be starting to take things personally. The list on the next page can help. Make a copy of it and post it in a conspicuous place to remind you to listen to yourself.

LISTEN FOR THESE SIGNALS

Be on the alert for the following statements. They are your warning lights that you may be starting to take things personally.

1. "How can you soar with eagles when you are cooped up with turkeys?"

2. "You don't know the people I work with."

3. "It's not that easy."

4. "Do you know what he/she said?"

5. "They didn't even..."

6. "I don't have to..."

7. "They never..."

8. "They always..."

9. "No one appreciates me."

10. "I don't get paid enough to take things professionally."

If you ever hear yourself saying any of the above, you are taking things personally. You can reduce your stress by learning to take the situation more professionally. The following page will provide practical ways to build your skill in this important area.

Save Time by Taking Situations Professionally

The practical approach of taking conflicts professionally will save you time. You will have fewer pieces to pick up after you calm down. You will learn to think better at challenging moments and increase your chances of doing things right the first time. You will develop better concentration because you do not have nagging thoughts such as, "They should have…" or "I should have…" Allowing your feelings to get in the way interrupts your thinking. Learning how to react professionally to the experiences you encounter helps you understand the bigger picture.

A Paid Professional

One savvy representative explained how he taught himself to take things professionally when dealing with difficult people. He reminded himself at key moments, "I am being paid to do this job. That means I am a professional. Those with whom I deal don't have to like me. I don't have to like them, but I make my living by handling people professionally and will learn something every time I encounter a difficult situation."

You may find that the people inside your organization are the toughest to handle. Even those who know how to handle outside customers with skill and respect are sometimes totally insensitive to others on the inside.

Whatever the situation, there are ways to identify potential frustrations. The next page will provide one suggestion about how to handle a difficult person.

Keep the Spotlight on the Issue

When you run into a difficult person, give yourself some perspective. Keep the spotlight away from yourself and on the issue at hand.

Techniques for Keeping the Spotlight on the Issue

❖

Rather Than:	Replace With:
"He is accusing me of making a mistake."	"How can we solve this situation?"
"She can't talk to me like that."	"Will you please tell me what needs to be done?"
"You're not perfect. You make mistakes too."	"This isn't the kind of service we want to provide. What can we do to correct this situation?"

CHAPTER
2

— RECAP OF TECHNIQUES —

Check the key concepts with which you agree.

I AGREE THAT:

❑ Some of the biggest challenges center on the people part of my job.

❑ The toughest people with whom I must deal are often those inside the organization.

❑ The best way to handle people and customers inside and outside the organization is to take each situation professionally and not personally.

For Reinforcement Say to Yourself:

"This is my job, and I like it.
Not because it is easy. Not because there are no difficult people.
Not because there are no frustrations. People are a part of any job.
So I make things easier for myself by taking things professionally."

❖

Taking things professionally and not personally pays off, but it takes energy and concentration. And it is often a change. When we are faced with the demands and changes of working in today's economy, it is easy to let ourselves get into a burnout condition. For these reasons, the next chapter gives you an easy way to spot burnout. It also gives specific ways to prevent burnout.

CHAPTER

3

Burnout–Threat to Customer Satisfaction

Eight Ways to Spot It, Five Ways to Prevent It

P R E V I E W

Burnout is a major threat to customer satisfaction. If you allow yourself to burn out, you will not be able to do your best thinking on the job. And you will lack reserves on which you can call when you experience periods of high demand.

Read the eight warnings signs of burnout on page 23 and pinpoint specific signals that apply to you or your situation. By recognizing potential problems early you will be able to begin working on them before they become difficult to resolve. You may want to keep a list of your general and specific warnings signs in some handy place like the inside of your medicine chest.

You can prevent burnout in five powerful ways that will be explained in the pages ahead.

Burnout is common, but it is not mandatory.*

❖

* For more information on job burnout, see **Preventing Job Burnout**, by Beverly Potter (Crisp Publications, 1996).

Eight Common Signs of Burnout

"I knew what to do, I just didn't feel like doing it," explained a technician about a complaint that erupted late one afternoon.

This statement pinpoints a symptom of job burnout—knowing what to do but not getting around to doing it. If you allow yourself to get into a burnout condition, you will not think or act as effectively as you could.

Burnout is a major threat to customer satisfaction because so much of what satisfies customers is positive action based on common sense and job interest. If you have let yourself get into a burnout condition, you may not do what you know it takes to satisfy a customer.

Several conditions make burnout particularly dangerous when you work with others. Some examples include:

- **When your work focuses mainly on problems or negatives**

- **When you rarely hear from people when you are doing a good job**

- **When one situation explodes into a problem and a regular customer forgets all of the good work accomplished in previous transactions**

As you read the eight warning signs on the next page, think about which apply to you. Also think about which may apply to others with whom you work. Would someone with whom you work benefit by being more aware of any of the signs listed?

REVIEW THE SIGNS

To help keep yourself aware of the signs leading to burnout, review the list of symptoms below and check any that apply to you. Post it on your medicine cabinet or some other handy place where you will see it on a regular basis.

Review this list the first of each month. This will help you recognize burnout signs in their early stages. This is the easiest time to get yourself back on track.

AM I:	YES	NO
1. Communicating less with others?	❏	❏
2. Feeling less energy?	❏	❏
3. Achieving lower productivity?	❏	❏
4. More often late for work or appointments?	❏	❏
5. Having trouble going to sleep and then waking up at night? Or wanting to sleep all the time?	❏	❏
6. Experiencing unplanned weight loss or gain?	❏	❏
7. Preoccupied with my health?	❏	❏
8. Experiencing decreased wants? Showing apathy and a drop in interest in what is happening in the world around me?	❏	❏

Additional Signs of Burnout

In addition to some of the eight common signals, you probably have less-common signals that can warn you of burnout.

The key is to know which of the eight signs relate to you and also know which other signs can alert you that burnout may be on the path. This way you can spot the possibility of burnout much earlier and get out of it more easily.

People have shared the following less-common signs. Use the list to stimulate your thinking and help you identify you own less-common, but very important, signs of burnout. Another good way to identify these signals is to ask the people who know you well. They can often tell you without hesitation.

❏ Decreased Concentration

You may find yourself standing by a file drawer. You knew you walked over to get something, but once you are there you cannot remember what. Decreased concentration also is the culprit when you become susceptible to interruptions from others and even yourself. It's easy to see how this can hurt doing the follow-through parts of customer satisfaction.

❏ A Short Fuse

Little things that you usually take in stride may become major irritants. Traffic may bug you, even when you are in no particular hurry. Or you might snap at a sales clerk who was busy with another customer.

❏ Suspicion of Joy

You see someone happy and whistling and think, "What a phony. It's not normal to feel like that all of the time."

❏ Complaining

You repeatedly express negative feelings. People around you think, "Here it comes, just like a tape recorder going on and on complaining about the same things again."

❏ Use of Artificial Stimulants

You find yourself taking an extra drink after work, drinking more coffee or tea or taking diet pills or other artificial stimulants. If this begins to happen, it is a major signal to examine what is going on in your life.

DISCOVER YOUR EARLY WARNING SIGNS

By staying alert it is possible to warn yourself in advance of a potential problem situation. Use the space below to pinpoint any general or specific signs that you may be on the way to burnout. Refer to the checklists on pages 23-24 to create this list.

Following Are My Signs of Burnout:

1. _____

2. _____

3. _____

4. _____

5. _____

Five Techniques for Preventing Burnout

Learning to detect the symptoms of job burnout is an important step in maintaining the positive action needed to satisfy customers. Another powerful tool is learning to stop those symptoms before they begin to surface. The following are five powerful techniques that you can use to prevent burnout from disrupting your work, your attitude and your ability to serve customers effectively:

1. **Exercise Daily**

2. **Take Care of Your Own Needs**

3. **Work Toward Measurable Targets**

4. **Say What You Feel, Directly and Skillfully**

5. **Do Good Things for Your Spirit**

Burnout Prevention 1: Exercise Daily

The number-one way to prevent or overcome burnout wins no popularity contest with those who are feeling run down. Frankly, it is the last thing we want to do when we are feeling frayed around the edges. The best solution, however, is physical exercise.

Oxygen is the reason most feelings of burnout disappear after physical exercise. When you exercise, you stimulate the flow of oxygen to your brain. Without ample oxygen, your thinking ability drops. The eight-cylinder engine of your mind begins operating on only four cylinders.

If you go home from work feeling tense and drained, even though you do not have a physically demanding job, ask yourself how to beat this feeling. Believe it or not, exercise is the best way to prevent the feelings of burnout. It is also a vital part of escaping from burnout. Some counselors will not see a client until that person has undertaken an exercise program.

You do not need to run a marathon. Simply walking two miles a day will do it. There are even some painless alternatives such as watching television as you bounce on a running trampoline, or wearing a Walkman as you run or walk.

You deserve to feel good. You deserve to think at your best. Create time to exercise regularly. Other burnout tactics will not be as effective until you exercise and stimulate the vital flow of oxygen to your brain on a daily basis.

Burnout Prevention 2: Take Care of Your Own Needs

Nationally known teacher of behavioral medicine and faculty member of the Louisiana State University Medical Center/Shreveport, Paul D. Ware, M.D., points out the following important considerations to avoid resenting being of service to others:

Taking care of your own needs and wants:

- **without devaluing yourself**

- **without devaluing others**

- **and, without devaluing the situation**

Devaluing yourself might involve an overweight person using a double banana split as a reward.

Devaluing others might involve an individual who refuses to answer a co-worker's ringing telephone.

Devaluing the situation might involve goofing off when a person is being paid to work.

Some examples of taking care of your own needs and wants include:

- ✔ **Making sure your good ideas get attention even if it takes speaking up several times, or putting your ideas in writing**

- ✔ **Asking people to notice your work accomplishments rather than hoping they will notice**

- ✔ **Asking directly for what you want, rather than feeling resentful because someone did not provide it without your asking**

Five Techniques for Preventing Burnout (CONTINUED)

Burnout Prevention 3: Work Toward Measurable Targets

Probe into a burnout condition and you will frequently find a lack of direction and no measurable targets.

Without measurable targets, it is difficult to achieve a sense of accomplishment. In too many jobs, workers hear nothing if things are going well. This is a poor situation because most people feel the need to be appreciated.

The reality is that in problem-oriented work, your telephone will never ring off the hook with people calling to express appreciation. The service you provide is expected. There are ways to compensate for this lack of unsolicited positive reinforcement, however. Working with specific targets can help you appreciate the quality of work that is being accomplished.

TARGETS HELP YOU APPRECIATE YOUR ACCOMPLISHMENTS

Even if no one notices your contribution, you can compliment yourself for meeting meaningful, measurable targets. Here is an example:

A woman responsible for writing up orders confessed, "I opposed standards and objectives before we established some targets, but I have changed my mind. They work."

"Here's my evidence," she added with a smile as she displayed perfectly shaped fingernails. "I used to chew my nails wondering how I was doing. Now I realize that when I complete at least 12 orders a day, my supervisor feels I'm doing a good job. I compliment myself. I don't worry if my supervisor hasn't counted them that day. Simply knowing I'm making a contribution has made me feel good about what I do."

TARGETS TURN ON YOUR CREATIVITY

If you are simply told how to do something and then left alone, it is easy to get bored and lose interest. On the other hand, when what you are achieving is explained and you are told why is it important, you will feel like you are making a contribution. Once you know the purpose of your job, you are less likely to make mistakes because you know why something is being done. Once you understand your role, you are in a position to think of ways to accomplish it even more efficiently by using your creativity.

TARGETS MAKE YOUR JOB EASIER

For many, a few encouraging words about "keeping everybody happy" is the extent of the customer satisfaction training. This, of course, is not very helpful. Some people will never be happy no matter what you provide for them. Others will not be happy about anything on a particular day. It is not realistic to have as the only target a general "keep everybody happy." Instead, request or give yourself the energizing direction of specific objectives.

Sample Targets to Stimulate Your Thinking

20 service requests completed a day

80 error-free document pages prepared a day

8 recommendations adopted a week

Average daily sales at your station of over $800

20 vouchers audited a day

20 purchase requests placed a day

On-time performance of 100 percent

Add your own:

_____

_____

_____

_____

_____

Five Techniques for Preventing Burnout (CONTINUED)

YOU CAN DESIGN YOUR TARGETS

Although targets will help prevent burnout and make jobs more enjoyable, designing them is not always easy. The following is an example of how a creative woman learned to make her job as a server in a conference facility more interesting.

"I make it a game," Debbie explained. "The first day of a two-day seminar, I check on the coffee and danishes several times to make sure there is plenty of each. I want to make sure each group has enough but not too much. On the second day, based on what the group devoured the first day, my goal is for there to be one danish left over before lunch. If there are no danishes left, someone might have wanted one and it wasn't available. If more than one is left, we have wasted some food."

While Debbie's target is unique to her job, her creativity is an inspiration. Designing targets for a service responsibility is more challenging than for production or sales jobs. Service is reactive. It is less predictable. But having measurable targets will help anyone, regardless of job, prevent burnout.

You may be thinking, "But I would feel even more burned out if I had targets and did not meet them." This does sound logical. However, there are some surprising results. Knowing where you stand is a powerful burnout prevention factor. Most people want to know specifically where they stand rather than having a vague notion of how they are doing. Also, targets can always be adjusted up or down as reality dictates.

In the space below describe a target that you either use or could use to make your work more valuable and challenging.

_____

_____

_____

_____

_____

Burnout Prevention 4:
Say What You Feel, Directly and Skillfully

You may be inclined to point out that saying what you feel is not always easy. It is not. Once you learn how and when to do it, however, it is a valuable skill with tremendous benefits. Like any skill, practice will make it easier.

Getting It Out

Pick one work situation where you have felt upset, but didn't communicate it to anyone directly. Give the situation a title and jot down a few sentences in the space provided describing the situation:

Work Situation Title: _____

Description: _____

_____

You will be asked to return to this situation after you explore some of the complications of communicating directly, which are presented in the next few pages.

BURNOUT AND COMPLAINING–
AVOID THE TEMPTATION

Have you ever been tempted to tell Person B about a problem situation that you are having with Person A? Tempting, isn't it? But if you tell Person B, you may notice that your relief is only temporary. Even though you spent time telling Person B about the problem, normally that individual is not in a position to solve it for you. Chances are Person A may never know how frustrating you find the situation with him or her unless you involve that person directly.

We do not get a sense of closure when we tell the wrong person. We therefore maintain our urge to tell someone else or to repeat ourselves. Check this out for yourself.

Can you think of someone who complained to you about someone else and then expressed the same complaint over and over? Such a scene is time-wasting and very tiring. Also, the problem never seems to get solved. When you say what you feel directly, even if it is not easy, it will clear the air and you will feel more energized.

Five Techniques for Preventing Burnout (CONTINUED)

Simply being direct is not enough. Your communication needs to be delivered with skill. Blurting out exactly what you feel will normally not serve you or the other person. Neither will an amateurish, "You make me mad." Find the right time. Use the right skills. The next several pages of this book will help you learn how to communicate directly and skillfully.

GIVE YOURSELF A HEAD START

Think about the situation you have not communicated, which you described on the previous page. Using the streamlined format listed below will help you practice a response so you will be ready the next time a situation similar to the one you described occurs.

"I feel frustrated about...
(specific observable event)

_____

_____ ."

"Will you please...
(specific observable action)

_____

_____

_____ ."

Rehearsing what you will say out loud to yourself helps. So does saying it into a tape recorder. Best of all, if possible, practice your planned response with someone who respects you but is not directly involved in the situation. Ask for feedback about the reasonableness of your message and your voice tone.

Do not lose momentum. When the situation crops up again, think about what you want to say and then communicate directly with the person involved.

Commit yourself to saying what you feel directly and skillfully. Develop your skill through practice. Other people will appreciate it and respect you for it. You will also feel better. Every time you are successful at direct communication, the easier it becomes to do it again. You are preventing burnout when you communicate directly.

Burnout Prevention 5: Do Good Things for Your Spirit

Learn how to keep yourself positive and motivated.* Discover those things that add energy and a lift to your day. Often these are small acts that you control. They might be as simple as using a favorite pen or pencil, sharing a joke with a co-worker or having soft music playing in the background.

Spirit Raisers

In the space provided below, make a list of your "spirit raisers." You do not have to show this list to anyone, so turn on your creativity.

What are some good things that you can do for your spirit on company time? Include items that will not disrupt your productivity or distract those around you.

1. _____
2. _____
3. _____
4. _____

What are some good things that you can do for your spirit on your own time? Include things that take less than three minutes or that do not cost any money.

1. _____
2. _____
3. _____
4. _____

* For an excellent book on staying positive and motivated, read **Attitude: Your Most Priceless Possession** by Elwood N. Chapman (Crisp Publications, 1995).

CHAPTER
3

─── R E C A P   O F   T E C H N I Q U E S ───

Check the techniques that you plan to use to prevent job burnout.

I WILL:

❏ Post a note with the eight general signs of burnout and/or my personal signs

❏ Exercise daily

❏ Take care of my own needs and wants without devaluing myself, others, or the situation

❏ Define some measurable personal targets and work to achieve them

❏ Do good things for my spirit

❏ Say what I feel directly and skillfully

For Reinforcement Say to Yourself:

"Even though burnout is common, it is not mandatory.
I take care of myself so that I keep myself up, energetic and thinking clearly."

❖

Another good way to reduce the probability of burnout is to encourage cooperation with others in your organization. Take steps to build cooperation, and you will make your job less stressful and more satisfying. The next section pinpoints a powerful way to generate needed cooperation.

CHAPTER

4

The Secret to Getting More Cooperation

Treat Each Person as a Customer

PREVIEW

Cooperation makes a real difference when you are working with customers. It makes the difficult easier.

Yet we often do not get the cooperation that we want because we believe that cooperation is given rather than earned.

The secret to getting more cooperation is to treat each person in your organization as well as you would an important customer.

This approach turns work into satisfying partnerships.

❖

Updating Your Beliefs

"There is no cooperation around here."

This indictment echoes across organization after organization. A lack of cooperation in any organization will invite burnout, drain energies, waste time and lower the quality of the work. On the other hand, working in a place where a spirit of cooperation exists makes the day go better and the work go more smoothly.

Everyone is in favor of cooperation. There is no argument with this statement. Why then, do we not have more cooperation at work? The reality is that it is often because of some out-of-date beliefs.

A Close Look at Cooperation

Indicate how you feel about the following by circling **A** for *agree* or **D** for *disagree* after each statement.

1. "I can count on people giving me cooperation because it is   A   D
    part of their job."

2. "I need to do things to earn cooperation."   A   D

3. "Some people are cooperative and others aren't."   A   D

4. "I can do things to increase the probability of   A   D
    each person being cooperative toward me."

If you agree with items two and four, you understand that these are more realistic ways to approach gaining cooperation from others.

Cooperation is earned more frequently than it is given.

A Selfish and Successful Strategy for Getting More Cooperation

How can you earn better cooperation? The people who seem to get the most cooperation are very quiet about their strategy. Yet as you study those who reap a rich harvest of cooperation, you will discover the following strategy at work. Those who are most successful have learned the following essential technique.

FOR COOPERATIVE PARTNERSHIPS, TREAT EACH PERSON AS A CUSTOMER

This strategy simply redirects skills you already use with customers outside your organization. To get more of what you want, treat each person inside your organization the same as an important external customer would be treated. When you do, you are guaranteed to get more cooperation.

Even though this approach seems like common sense, there are five major barriers to using it, which are listed on the next few pages.

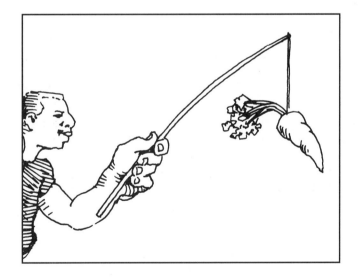

Roadblocks to Avoid

Roadblock 1: "He isn't a customer: He is just someone I work with."

You recognize this attitude if you have ever observed the following: The telephone rings. An individual answers it with an upbeat tone. You can almost hear the musical notes and see the rosebuds. Suddenly there is a change. The person who picked up the phone has discovered that the caller is someone inside the organization. The rosebuds disappear. The voice is now a flat and expressionless, "Oh, it's you."

No wonder people feel drained at the end of the day. It is hard to feel essential when you hear, "Oh it's you."

Consider another situation. How many times have you wanted to provide service to someone outside of your organization—only to find yourself blocked by someone inside? Needed information is missing. An important telephone call is not returned. A specially requested delivery date was ignored.

You will find you will get more of what you want from people inside your organization when you learn to treat each one as you would treat an important customer.

Roadblock 2: "But you don't know the people I work with."

This is true. No one else fully understands the day-to-day demands that you encounter. No one appreciates the creativity and energy you invest to get your work done through people. No other person understands the nuances and complexities of the people with whom you work.

What we all do understand is this: The more complicated the people aspects of your work, the more interpersonal skill it takes to get what you want. In today's economy, we all experience demands for higher productivity. Many of us are in an unforgiving economic climate with little acceptance of explanations about why a job was not done to expectations.

The more difficult people are to work with, the more you benefit by treating each person as a customer.

Roadblock 3: "I don't have time."

Treating everyone as you would a customer will actually save you time. This is where the productive selfishness comes in. You probably know someone who talks down to those with less glamorous jobs, such as in the mailroom, with the attitude, "I don't have to treat those turkeys well." Have you noticed how that person's mail often takes longer to arrive than it takes to get mail to a person using a more respectful style?

Human nature suggests that if you treat someone disrespectfully, sooner or later that person will find a way to get even with you: "But I thought you said…", "I was only doing what she told me," or "Did you see what he did?"

Save yourself the irritation of someone "getting even" sooner or later. It only takes a few seconds more to treat each person as a customer now, and it could save you some nasty surprises in the future.

Roadblock 4: "But this approach doesn't always work."

You are right. Nothing in life always works. What you need to do is work with the odds. Nothing as complicated as dealing with people can be handled with one technique. Use approaches that have the highest probability of success for you but always have a handful of Plan B techniques ready in case Plan A does not work.

Roadblock 5: "Why should I? I'm the customer."

It is a paradox. Even though you are a customer and deserve respectful and competent treatment, you will get more of what you want if you take the lead. Treat the other person respectfully. Listen. Communicate in ways that make things easier for the other person. Do all the things that a traditional supplier should do. You will not feel guilty afterwards. On the contrary, you will increase the probability of that person wanting to work again with you. Treating someone skillfully pays real dividends. The signals you send out are usually similar to those that are returned.

MORE ROADBLOCKS TO SUCCESS

Simple? YES. Easy? NO. Treat each person as a customer. It sounds simple, but it is not always easy.

Look at the following list of attitudes that function as additional roadblocks. Check any you have heard or perhaps even said:

❏ **"I'm not good with people. You are either born good with people, or you are not."**

❏ **"It's not my job."**

❏ **"I tried it once. It didn't work."**

❏ **"My situation is different."**

❏ **"No one trained me."**

❏ **"People I work with don't care how it gets done. They just want results."**

❏ **"I know all of this already."**

❏ **"It's not that easy."**

Can you think of some other roadblocks you have heard? Write them here:

❏ _____

❏ _____

❏ _____

❏ _____

❏ _____

Which of the above roadblocks might be robbing you of the rewards of smooth-working relationships? Check any that apply. Then when you hear the offending words, recognize them as barriers and take counter-action. It is a good time to turn on your creativity, so that roadblocks will not stop you from getting the results you want.

Working as Partners–
Treating Your Boss as a Customer

To save yourself time, treat your boss as you would a valued customer.

Although some might say that to treat your boss as a customer is wrong, think of the idea from a different perspective. If you were in the boss's shoes, would you value being treated with the respect that an important customer receives?

There is an old saying that applies to this situation: "What goes around, comes around." Get more respect and save yourself time, by applying your customer satisfaction skills to your boss.

CASE STUDY
Blair and the New Boss

Blair's new job was only two months old, and she was disappointed already. Her new boss just did not seem to notice her. It seemed like her new boss was always in meetings and Blair never had a chance to sit down and go over problems with her.

One afternoon as Blair's boss was leaving for a meeting, she stopped by Blair's desk, sat down and looked at her straight in the eyes and said: "Blair, I get the feeling that you think I should go home at night and ask myself, 'How can I make Blair's job easier?' Well, I don't. What I want you to do is to go home at night and ask yourself, 'How can I make my boss's job easier?'"

For several minutes after Blair's boss left, Blair sat thinking. She was irritated. She did not like to believe that what her boss said was true, but she knew it was.

The day Blair started treating her boss as an important customer, she started feeling better and getting more of what she wanted.

Blair began to notice that when she asked her boss something, she often did not get an answer. But when she wrote a note with the same kind of question, sooner or later she always got that note back with an answer written across it. When Blair learned her boss responded better to written inquiries, Blair stopped the corridor questioning. Blair also noticed that her boss asked her two or three times if she had finished things, even though Blair had already told her yes, she had. Then Blair decided she would write a brief note for her boss each day, describing what had been accomplished.

Now that Blair has made her boss's job easier, her boss has begun to single Blair out and tell others what a good job Blair is doing. This positive feedback has helped Blair become a more productive employee who enjoys her job more.

Working as Partners–Treating Your Boss as a Customer (CONTINUED)

TREAT YOUR BOSS AS A CUSTOMER

Some Questions for You

Why might some people hesitate to do this?

1. _____

2. _____

3. _____

How can it save you time to treat your boss as you would an important customer?

_____

What are some other practical reasons to treat your boss as a customer?

_____

_____

_____

TREAT CO-WORKERS AS CUSTOMERS, TOO

When you see each person as a customer, you will enjoy more cooperation. You will be using the skills that you used to reserve for people outside the organization, in new ways, with new advantages to you.

"BUT I DON'T HAVE CUSTOMERS"

Listed below are nine observations that cover the gamut of concerns you might have about adopting this or any new customer satisfaction strategy.

Please circle each statement: **A** for agree or **D** for disagree

1. People who talk with those outside of our organization are the only ones who have responsibility for customer satisfaction. A D

2. "Client" is often a good term to substitute for "customer." A D

3. People will understand if you are having a down day and are more temperamental than normal. A D

4. If a person knows how to do something well, they will automatically do it well every time. A D

5. If something does not feel natural, you automatically should not do it. A D

6. Your situation may be different, and you do not have customers. A D

7. If you use a new idea once and it does not work, never use it again. A D

8. Learning customer skills may require the kind of discipline and practice that is common in becoming an accomplished athlete. A D

9. Every time you pick up the telephone, you are your organization. A D

See author's answers on page 116 to determine the extent to which you might be erecting barriers to using the strategies outlined in this chapter.

CHAPTER
4

RECAP OF TECHNIQUES

To get the most out of this chapter, check techniques that you plan to use more frequently.

I WILL:

❏ Update my beliefs about cooperation. Cooperation is earned more frequently than it is given.

❏ Build cooperative partnerships by treating each person as a customer both inside and outside my organization.

❏ Save myself time by treating my boss as a very important customer.

For Reinforcement Say to Yourself:

"Even if it is not easy, I treat each person during my workday as a customer. It always pays off. I get better cooperation. And I get the satisfaction of working as a partner."

❖

As you gain the benefits of treating each person as a customer, it is a natural step to want to refine your ability to handle customers. The next section will explore a subtle but important refinement: moving beyond customer service to customer satisfaction.

PART

2

BUILDING
THE
FOUNDATION

The Problem with Customer Service

Aim for Satisfaction

PREVIEW

You shortchange both yourself and your customers if you are content simply to provide customer service. To do a superior job it will be necessary for you to go beyond service to customer satisfaction.

Customer service is defined by the supplier.
Customer satisfaction is defined by the customer.

This important but subtle difference, once understood, will build motivation, creativity and commitment.

By establishing specific targets—and achieving them—you will forge the way for motivated customer satisfaction.

A practical system for negotiating mutually agreed upon targets begins with identifying what you and your customer want and need. Then you determine how well you can supply them.

Concentrating on satisfaction and learning how to deliver it will prevent burnout, build confidence and stimulate more satisfaction for both you and your customers.

❖

Satisfaction Is Defined by the Customer

"I give good service. The customers just don't appreciate it."

This statement pinpoints the subtle danger of concentrating on customer service alone. Such concentration loses the vital focus of what satisfies the customer—inside or outside the organization.

Why Satisfaction Is Better than Service

Think of your response if a waiter walked to your restaurant table and announced, "You had a great dinner!" You would probably smile at such a scenario because you are accustomed to a situation in which the waiter would ask, "How did you enjoy your dinner?" In this situation, the server lets you decide how satisfied you are, rather than telling you what he thinks.

This scene illustrates the difference between service and customer satisfaction. Customer service is provider-defined rather than customer-defined, whereas customer satisfaction must always be defined by the customer.

Do not stop at customer service. Go beyond service to customer satisfaction.

CASE STUDY
Tom and the Two-Hour Trouble

Six months ago, if you had asked Tom, a maintenance technician, if he provided good service, he would have given you a quick "yes." He did give a good service. He concentrated on doing his job well. He enjoyed being a technician and took pride in being technically perfect.

But when Tom began to learn about customer satisfaction, he made a change. He used to say that a certain type repair in two hours was "doggone good service." Now he is more sensitive to what his customers regard as "doggone good service." By asking them, he has learned that some expect a progress report every 30 minutes, while others simply want to know when the repair is completed.

When Tom learned to concentrate on customer satisfaction, he found it made a positive difference, which showed up in the number of compliments he received. Tom still provides excellent customer service but spends time with each of his clients to ensure there is customer satisfaction as well.

Meet the Requirements of the People You Serve

Assume that you are eating lunch when a co-worker from another group sits down next to you. Before you have taken your first bite, you start to hear a barrage: "Do you know what happened? This morning someone had the nerve to complain about some work I did for him. I know my job. I've been in it for years. I do good work. What does he know? I'm the expert."

Now, ask yourself the following questions:

- **What would I say to this person?**

- **Why might someone believe that they define the value of their work rather than allowing the customer to define it?**

- **What techniques could my co-worker use to take criticism professionally and not personally?**

- **What are three personal advantages of satisfying the customer's requirements?**

Customer Satisfaction Is Easier When You Have Targets

If you are tempted to say that your situation is different, that specific targets are difficult to define for your job or that targets have no value, consider a different perspective. Teenagers who may have difficulty staying motivated in their studies often can concentrate for hours on a video game. The secret is that these games have specific targets where players can continually measure how they are doing. They receive frequent feedback about how well their objective is being met. Video games are only one example. The reason that bowling, golf, baseball and other sports attract us is because they all have targets and ways of "keeping score."

TARGETS BY ANY NAME

Organizations also "keep score."* They use different terms to describe the desired results, but the purpose is to determine how they are doing. Are you aware of targets in your daily work? Do any of the following names sound familiar? Check those that apply to your situation:

- ❑ **Requirements**

- ❑ **Expectations**

- ❑ **Goals**

- ❑ **Objectives**

- ❑ **Other:** _____

The meanings of the terms listed above are not always the same. Check with your manager to make sure you have the precise definition of any term used to measure your accomplishments. Working toward targets by any name will make your job easier and more satisfying.

---

* For two excellent books on "keeping score," see *Effective Performance Appraisals* by Robert Maddux (Crisp Publications, 1993) and *Personal Performance Contracts* by Roger Fritz (Crisp Publications, 1993).

WHO ESTABLISHES YOUR TARGETS?

Think about your situation. Check the box beside the statement that best describes your targets, goals or objectives:

- ❑ **You provide your targets.**

- ❑ **Targets are established by your manager.**

- ❑ **Targets are determined by input from both you and your manager.**

- ❑ **Targets include customer input as well as input from both you and your manager.**

Which statement do you think will lead to customer satisfaction? Write why you feel this way in the space provided below:

_____

_____

_____

When the Target is Provided by Your Manager

The following advice will help you get more satisfaction if your manager has been responsible for providing your customer service targets.

MAKE SURE YOU KNOW THE PURPOSE OF THE TARGET

Once you fully understand the target, you will be able to explain problems that may be unique to your customers. If you do this effectively, you will have less stress and will be in a position to speak for your organization. It sometimes takes asking questions of others, but it is worth it. Ask enough questions of customers and co-workers and then share what you have learned with your manager. This will help both of you understand and define the customer service targets that are part of your job.

Customer Satisfaction Is Easier
When You Have Targets (continued)

When You Help Define the Target

Work will be much easier once people, including those inside your organization and in your personal life, articulate specifically what they expect and what would satisfy them. Some do not know what they want or need. Others hope you will guess their needs without having to tell you. (This is particularly true in personal relationships.) Consider how illogical this statement is: "If you have to tell people what you want, it doesn't really count." It is up to you to help others define their expectations.

There may be some additional complications when finding out specifically what people expect and require. For example, you may face any of these situations:

- **You may know more about your specialty than the other person. They may not know enough to be able to ask for what they want.**

- **You may be working in a rapidly changing environment where expectations have not been clearly spelled out for anyone.**

- **You may be simply one person in a chain handling a service or product and may never even see or talk with the end user.**

Although it is not always easy to define specific expectations and requirements, it is worth the effort to discover as much as you can and communicate your findings with others who are involved.

A Shortcut for Defining Targets

Keep the diagram presented below in mind as you listen and ask questions.

A great place to start is to determine what the customer wants and does not want and what your organization wants and does not want, and then to align these elements. Many people start with what they do not want. Use this instead to uncover what they do want.

Start with the four corners, then determine the target.

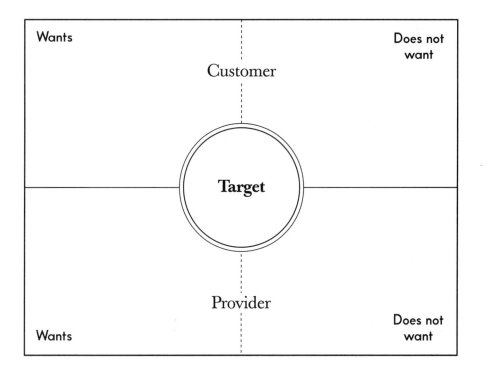

ARM YOURSELF WITH WRITTEN TARGETS

Even though writing specific targets, expectations or requirements may seem cumbersome, it is a surprisingly effective time-saver. When starting a new project at work, it is easy to nod in agreement that you understand what the target is. This is usually an optimistic conclusion based on the excitement of starting something new. How many times have you been on a committee and when someone wrote a summary following the group discussion, and later circulated it, the response was "That's not what I said" or "That's not what I wanted?"

Think about your personal life. How many times have you hinted to someone about something you wanted only to have your friend or spouse miss the hint entirely?

In organizations, putting expectations in writing ensures that you and the other person have the best possible understanding of the outcome that you both want. By encouraging feedback, you prevent misunderstandings later.

Write some major specific targets that relate to customer satisfaction in your organization.

_____

_____

_____

_____

_____

_____

The Pleasant Payoff

At first, it may seem time-consuming to generate written expectations. It may well slow things at the beginning, but you will be pleasantly surprised by how written targets and expectations will pay off.

Written targets will prevent rework. They will also prevent the frustration of not knowing the purpose of what you need to do. Your personal satisfaction will increase because you have a better handle on what your customer wants. You will also reduce the possibility of resentments because you do not get what you want.

AIM FOR SATISFACTION

Answer each of the following questions by circling each statement **A** for *agree* or **D** for *disagree*. If possible, discuss your responses with your manager.

1. There are some people whom you just cannot please. A D

2. Once you are experienced in working with customers, you automatically know what they want without having to check. A D

3. Customers are always satisfied when you do a good job. A D

4. You feel less stress when you understand customer expectations. A D

5. You feel less stress when you check with customers to see how satisfied they are. A D

6. All employees are entitled to know how well they are satisfying customers. A D

7. You waste less time and effort when you know specifically what the expectations of the customers are. A D

8. Customer feedback always helps make your job better in the long term. A D

9. Satisfying expectations is the key to meaningful relationships. A D

See author comments on page 116 to determine the extent to which you believe setting customer-centered targets leads to mutual satisfaction.

Customer Satisfaction

CHAPTER
5

RECAP OF TECHNIQUES

To get the most out of this chapter, check the concepts that you plan to use more frequently.

I WILL:

❑ Aim for customer satisfaction rather than merely customer service.

❑ Focus my work by using customer-centered targets.

❑ Understand the purpose of my customer-centered targets, regardless of how they are assigned.

❑ Make sure I can clearly explain all customer-centered targets.

❑ Work with my customer to define any vaguely defined targets.

❑ Avoid unnecessary rework by making sure that I have a specific direction based on written objectives whenever possible.

For Reinforcement Say to Yourself:

> *"Because I do not want to waste my time, I ask questions
> and listen to learn exactly what others expect from me.
> They appreciate it, and it makes my job easier."*

❖

Aiming for customer satisfaction, more than simply customer service, does make a difference in how you see people. It also makes it easier to tackle the topic of the next chapter, which explores the technique of solving problems without blaming.

CHAPTER
6

The Customer Is Not Always Right, But...

Solve Problems Without Blaming

P R E V I E W

THE VALUE OF PROBLEM SOLVING

It is true. The customer is not always right, but it is also true that the customer is always the customer. This means that solving the problem is often more important than determining who is "right." When someone is irritated, if you can solve the problem without blaming yourself or others, you will reduce stress, everyone will feel better and you will save time. You will be on your way to customer satisfaction.

STEPS TO PROBLEM SOLVING

You will be able to add to your problem-solving skills by using the seven practical steps that are presented later in this section. These are guaranteed to assist you in dealing with someone who is irritated.

❖

The Customer is Always the Customer

"I need this advice the most with people inside of our organization," a pressured technician confided as she pointed to the following saying posted to the side of her computer terminal:

The customer is not always right,
but the customer is always the customer.

The person who invented this saying deserves a vote of thanks from everyone who works with customers. Considerable time is saved when you learn to not get embroiled in a dialogue with yourself about whether a customer is right or wrong. It does not matter if the customer is right or wrong. What matters is that you are committed to providing your customer, whenever possible, with what he or she wants and needs. It is the relationship that matters. Not who is right.

To handle an irate person, solve the problem without blaming yourself or others.

Blaming– A Barrier to Problem Solving

"That's not my job."

"Nobody told me to…"

"That happened when I wasn't here."

You have heard these blaming statements enough to recognize what a waste of time they are. Have you noticed that after a person has vigorously blamed someone else, he or she ends up doing the job anyway. By then, however, not only has that person created a negative impression on the person to whom the statement was made, but valuable time has been wasted which could have been used solving the problem.

Blaming can also be turned inward. You may be the type of person who does not blame others but treats yourself in ways that you would never treat someone else. You may tell yourself:

"You dummy, you should have…"

"Why didn't you…?"

"You messed it up again."

Blaming yourself or blaming others are both unproductive. Blaming others wastes time and hurts relationships. Blaming yourself drains energy and often leads to procrastination. Solving problems without blaming is the remedy for both.

BELIEFS AS A BARRIER TO PROBLEM SOLVING

Various beliefs about problem solving can complicate our lives. We do not usually express these beliefs directly. We only reveal the edges, or outcomes. The following statements were designed to stimulate your thinking about the beliefs that may be a barrier to problem solving.

Uncover Your Beliefs About Problem Solving

Please circle either **A** if you *agree* or **D** if you *disagree* with the following statements.

1. If you did not cause the problem, you cannot be hurt by it.   A   D

2. If you can identify who caused the problem, you are excused from taking action to solve the problem.   A   D

3. If you did not cause the problem, it is inappropriate for you to help solve it.   A   D

4. If someone did not tell you what to do, you cannot be responsible for not doing it.   A   D

5. If you do not understand something, it is the other person's responsibility to make sure that you understand it.   A   D

6. If you do not understand something, it is your responsibility to make sure you do.   A   D

7. If the situation is unfair, you are not responsible for taking steps to improve it.   A   D

8. It is reasonable to expect that you will not be given a job until all customer expectations have been completely identified.   A   D

9. Defining work expectations and requirements is part of each person's job.   A   D

10. If someone else makes the mistake, you are not responsible for doing anything about it.   A   D

Discussing your answers with someone else will stimulate your thinking even further. Please read the author's recommended responses on page 116 of this book.

Shortcut to Stopping the Blame Habit

Avoid Being a Victim

Although a number of different beliefs lead to blaming, one strategy cures them all. That is to solve the problem and skip the blame.

You will be even further ahead when you prevent problems. When you prevent or solve problems, you can avoid the depressing habit of feeling like a victim. People who feel like victims often blame others and themselves. Their thinking generally runs: "No one told me to do that" or "I should have known."

CASE STUDY
Sandy Steps Out of the Victim Role

Sandy related the following situation and the personal benefits she realized.

"Well, my life has certainly changed! Maybe I should say that I changed my life.

"For the first year that I was in a specialized order entry job, I was always stressed and running behind. A person would call with a request at the last minute. I would drop everything and get busy on that request. And then somebody else would call and request something else. Some days were quiet, but on other days it seemed like everyone called. For a long time, I complained about other people not being organized. I convinced myself they were wrong to call at the last minute. They should be more understanding.

"Finally, I got tired of feeling like my back was always against the wall. I mentally assumed that people would call at the last minute. My strategy was to change what I was doing. I went through the records and put together a history for several of the last-minute requesters. After I isolated the buying history, I learned to predict with some accuracy when a person would order. I discovered some people called most frequently just before the 15th or the end of the month. Another always called on Friday afternoon. Once I figured out the pattern, I began calling them first. Calling on the 12th and 28th of each month gave me more lead time with those who ordered in mid-month or at the end of a month. Calling on Thursday afternoon helped with the Friday-afternoon caller.

"Basically, I stopped waiting for other people to change. I took action to make my situation better, and I feel great! Because I feel in more control, I have less stress."

Solving problem without blaming yourself or others means less stress, more time and more satisfaction. You can enjoy even more of these benefits by using the seven steps outlined on the next page.

Seven Practical Steps to Customer Problem Solving

Use the following seven steps to calm a person and get a solution under way. This section of the chapter will show you practical ways to put these steps to work for you. You can use them in order or pick the steps that relate the most to your situation.

Step 1.   **Express respect.**

"What you're telling me is important."

Step 2.   **Listen to understand.**

"Tell me what happened."

Step 3.   **Uncover the expectations.**

"Will you please tell me what you feel needs to be done?"

Step 4.   **Repeat the specifics.**

"Let me make sure I understand what you need..."

Step 5.   **Outline the solution or alternatives.**

"I will take this action" or "You have several choices..."

Step 6.   **Take action and follow through.**

"Your refund has been requested. I will personally check with Accounting to ensure your check goes out Friday."

Step 7.   **Double-check for satisfaction.**

"I'm following up to make sure your check arrived."

Step 1: Express Respect

When people are irritated, this is usually triggered by a feeling that their worth has not been recognized yet. Not recognizing someone's worth is often conveyed unintentionally.

Think about the following situation for a moment: Picture yourself walking into a department store. You know exactly what you want. You get the merchandise and walk to the cash register area, ready to pay. Two sales people are talking. Neither turns to recognize you. Instead, they continue discussing a party that they both attended last weekend. What are your feelings as you stand unattended? Chances are you are irritated. You may even put down the merchandise and go to another store. All because people did not bother to communicate your worth as a customer.

Expressing respect for a person and his or her situation will save you time and frustration.

When you are confronted with an irritated person, the best thing you can do is to quickly communicate respect. It is almost impossible for someone to be angry with you once you have expressed respect.

EXAMPLE TO STIMULATE YOUR THINKING

No single way of expressing respect works every time or with every person. Because of this, you should have five or six examples of calming language available for use at challenging moments. You may select your favorites from the list shown on the following pages, or you may develop your own. Experience is the best way to learn which work best with your customers.

CALMING LANGUAGE THAT EXPRESSES RESPECT

As you read the following statements, imagine how you would feel if they were said to you. Give each statement an "X" on a scale of 1 to 10. A 1 means you would be irritated, and a 10 means such a statement would be calming for you.

Using phrases like these does not take much time (see estimate in parentheses) and can actually save you time in the long run by keeping customers calm.

1. I will check into this right now. (2 seconds)

   1   2   3   4   5   6   7   8   9   10
   Irritating   Calming

2. This is important. (1 second plus)

   1   2   3   4   5   6   7   8   9   10
   Irritating   Calming

3. This isn't the kind of service we want to give you. (3 seconds)

   1   2   3   4   5   6   7   8   9   10
   Irritating   Calming

4. I apologize. (1 second)

   1   2   3   4   5   6   7   8   9   10
   Irritating   Calming

5. Thank you for letting me know about... (2 seconds plus)

   1   2   3   4   5   6   7   8   9   10
   Irritating   Calming

6. Your work is important to us. (2 seconds)

   1   2   3   4   5   6   7   8   9   10
   Irritating   Calming

7. Thank you for telling me about this. (2 seconds)

   1   2   3   4   5   6   7   8   9   10
   Irritating   Calming

8. **We want you to be pleased with our work. (2 seconds)**

    1   2   3   4   5   6   7   8   9   10

    Irritating   *Calming*

9. **Thank you for your patience. (2 seconds)**

    1   2   3   4   5   6   7   8   9   10

    Irritating   *Calming*

10. **Let me make some notes about what needs to be corrected. (3 seconds)**

    1   2   3   4   5   6   7   8   9   10

    Irritating   *Calming*

11. **I apologize for the inconvenience you have endured. (3 seconds)**

    1   2   3   4   5   6   7   8   9   10

    Irritating   *Calming*

12. **I want to serve you. (2 seconds)**

    1   2   3   4   5   6   7   8   9   10

    Irritating   *Calming*

Select Your Own Calming Statements

Which examples of calming language would you use? Pick those that fit your situation and the people with whom you work.

1. _____

_____

2. _____

_____

3. _____

_____

Seven Practical Steps to Customer Problem Solving (CONTINUED)

CASE STUDY
George

George was heard to say to a co-worker:

"If my manager thinks I'm going to tell someone, 'I want to serve you' then she is mistaken. I'm not people's servant, especially if they made the mistake. I am here to help them, but I'm certainly not here to serve them."

Questions for Discussion

1. How would you predict that George, or any person who expresses this, would feel at the end of a work day?

2. How satisfied do you think such an individual feels about work?

3. How would you rate this individual's likelihood of experiencing burnout?

Step 2: Listen to Understand

Have you ever been irritated and begun to explain your situation to someone who does not listen? If so, you know how frustrating it can be. For customer satisfaction, it is essential to listen for understanding. Listening also provides time to collect your thoughts.*

Listen for these vital areas in addition to what the person is saying:

What the person is feeling

What the person is wanting

What the person is thinking

Have you ever confronted someone who is angry, given them the exact answer they wanted and still had them rehash the original issue? People often do not listen well when they are irritated. You can count on it. People do not listen well when they are angry. What will open the door to improved listening on their part is your letting them know you understand how they feel.#

Listening to understand what people are wanting helps you understand what problem to solve. For example, one person might be irritated about the quality and another about the timing.

Listening for what they are thinking often reveals why they feel the way they do. Consider, for instance, the implications of the following remarks:

- **"I thought the material was going to be ready by noon today."**

- **"I knew you would mess up on this again, just like last time!"**

- **"I had no idea it was going to cost this much."**

- **"I am going to an important meeting and you don't have my materials ready."**

- **"The way I do my job doesn't count for much anyway."**

* For more information on listening, read **The Business of Listening** by Diane Bone (Crisp Publications, 1994).

This useful skill is covered in helpful detail in "Leadership Effectiveness Training" seminars and books. For more information contact Effectiveness Training, 531 Stevens Avenue, Solana Beach, California 92075.

Seven Practical Steps to Customer Problem Solving (CONTINUED)

CASE STUDY
The Benefits of Listening to Understand

Tom told a co-worker:

"I had heard about 'listening to understand' for years. But last Tuesday I decided to do it with every person with whom I came in contact. I was very pleased with the results.

"One customer who regularly calls has always bothered me because she is so abrupt and impatient even when I try to be friendly. On that Tuesday, we had a pause while waiting for some information, and we started talking personally. She mentioned that she was tired because she had been awakened at four a.m. by her mother, who was suffering from Alzheimer's disease. Her mother was trying to get dressed and was putting a sweater on her legs, like pants. My caller confessed how hard things had become because of her mother's disease.

"My impatience vanished. I began to understand why my caller was often irritable. It had nothing to do with me. It had to do with her family situation.

"I am going to practice listening to understand and try to get to know my customers better. I'm convinced it will make my job more satisfying."

Step 3: Uncover the Expectations

Careful, thoughtful listening will give you a good start toward understanding expectations. Asking the following questions can assist you in delving into what the person actually wants and needs.

Check those that you can use on your job, and use them as a basis to develop your own:

- ❑ "Please tell me what needs to be done."

- ❑ "How can we resolve this situation?"

- ❑ "What can we do right away to get this situation straightened out?"

- ❑ "Was there anything else that wasn't the way you wanted it?"

- ❑ "How can I assist you?"

Other questions you can use:

_____

_____

_____

_____

_____

_____

_____

Seven Practical Steps to Customer Problem Solving (CONTINUED)

Step 4: Repeat the Specifics

You benefit in two ways by repeating your understanding of a customer's expectations. You benefit because:

1. **You find out whether you understand exactly what the person wants.**

2. **People calm down once they realize you understand what they want.**

Two popular, but ineffective attempts to verify expectations are: "I know" or "I understand." These statements often inflame rather than calm. The reason is because we do not believe anyone can know or understand our exact situation.

Rather than saying, "I know," repeat the specifics in the form of a question. This verification gives evidence of understanding. Aim to have the other person say, "Yes, that's it. You understand."

Here are some examples:

"To make sure I am on the right track, let me double-check what you want."

"To prevent a problem, let me summarize what needs to happen."

"So the problem is..."

Step 5: Outline the Solution or Alternatives

Handling an irate person is easy when you can solve the problem. If you can, say so immediately.

The tough part is when you cannot give people exactly what they want. In this situation, outline the alternatives. The following are some examples of what you can say:

- "I will check into this right now and will get back to you before twelve."

- "Here is a possibility."

- "You can..."

- "We do have..."

- "There is an alternative."

If someone is irate, always have an alternative prepared. This will show your sincere interest in resolving the situation. Saying, "There is nothing I can do" will provoke some people into an attack mode.

The following are some examples of alternatives to use when you want to express care even though a solution is unlikely:

- "I will put a note on my calendar for Friday and will check again for you."

- "Sometimes our regional center has what you're looking for. I'll give them a call."

- "I will put your name on our mailing list in case something develops. In the meantime, I'll keep my eyes open for a possible replacement."

Seven Practical Steps to Customer Problem Solving (CONTINUED)

Step 6: Take Action and Follow Through

All the benefits discussed in the first five steps will be for naught if you do not take action, then follow through on your commitments. Follow-through occurs in two basic categories: immediate and later. We have all heard the saying, "Do it now." This is the best style for immediate resolution. In many instances, however, it is not possible to follow through immediately. Time is required. You may have more than one item to resolve.

Your major weapon to resolve problems by timely follow-through is your calendar or your wrist alarm.

If you tell a person you will get back to him or her before twelve o'clock, do it. If you tell someone you will call before four o'clock on Thursday, make a note in your calendar and do it.

If you have a wrist watch with a built-in alarm, it can be helpful to set it just prior to the time that action was promised to ensure that you have a professional follow-through.

Regardless of which method you choose, make a habit of following through!

Step 7: Double-Check for Satisfaction

Double-checking (or following up again) for satisfaction is such an essential step that an entire chapter is devoted to it later in this book. Chapter 8 provides tips on how to gather feedback from customers. This part of the book highlights why double-checking for satisfaction builds appreciation and loyalty. It is one of the secrets of customer satisfaction.

SOLVING PROBLEMS AND SELF-PROTECTION

The major reason to solve customer problems is for self-protection. This is particularly true when you deal with someone who is irritated. Helping solve the problem will save you time, reduce your stress and make you feel better. Even if you are not to blame for the problem and even if you do not have total control over the outcome, your best bet is still to help get the problem solved.

CHAPTER
6

—— RECAP OF TECHNIQUES ——

To get the most out of this chapter, check the techniques that you will benefit by using more frequently.

I WILL:

❑ Handle an irate person by solving the problem without blaming myself or others.

❑ Update any personal beliefs that are barriers to problem solving.

❑ Avoid feeling like a victim.

❑ Express respect, listen to understand, uncover expectations.

❑ Repeat specifics to verify that I understand what is expected.

❑ Outline the solution or present alternatives.

❑ Take action and follow through.

❑ Double-check for satisfaction.

For Reinforcement Say to Yourself:

"I solve problems without blaming myself or others.
It saves everyone time. It reduces stress, and it builds teamwork."

❖

Approaching problems in this positive way takes practice, but it is rewarding. The customer satisfaction techniques in the next part of this book are also well worth practicing. They will help you smooth out even the most challenging customer situations.

CHAPTER 7

Getting What You Want

Save Time with Proven Techniques

── PREVIEW ──

You will get what you want and also get more cooperation when you use the following techniques with people both inside and outside of your organization. You can also adapt the following six techniques to your personal life.

Make it easy for others to cooperate with you by using the following ideas:

PURPOSE	TECHNIQUE
To reduce irritation	Use a warm and cooperative tone of voice
To build confidence	Use "I will…"
To reduce frustration	Use "Will you…?"
To say no courteously	Use "You can…"
To save time	Give the reason first
To reduce tension	Call anyway

Perhaps you are already using some of these techniques part of the time. Enjoy the benefits of using all of them all of the time. You, your customers, your co-workers and your friends will appreciate the results. These techniques are explored in depth in this chapter.

❖

Make It Easy for Others to Cooperate with You

"I tried it once, and it didn't work. Besides, my situation is different."

You have probably heard the comment above a number of times. It is sad to hear. The belief that one attempt is enough or that a situation is just "different" robs people of personal satisfaction and costs organizations thousands of dollars each year.

Here is why: Excellence grows out of skillful practice. As you watch Olympic competitors on television, you often hear how each individual has practiced thousands of hours to compete for only a few seconds or minutes.

As driver of an automobile, you have practiced changing lanes, stopping and parking hundreds of times. Practice is how you master anything that you do well.

The belief that "my situation is different" often diverts people from working to improve a solution. Although it is true that each situation is unique, there are usually strong similarities.

Almost everything including customer relationship techniques needs to be tailored. If someone goes into a store to buy a jacket, chances are the sleeves need to be changed, some part taken in, another part shortened. It is the same with most customer satisfaction situations.

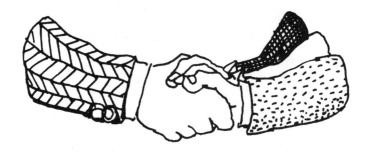

Six Cooperation Techniques

Even though there are differences in the various situations you face, you can always tailor problem-solving techniques to fit your personality, your pressures and your customers.

Enjoy even more cooperation by using the researched and proven techniques presented in this section. You, your co-workers and your customers will benefit.

1. **To reduce irritation, use a warm and cooperative tone of voice**

2. **To build confidence, use "I will..."**

3. **To reduce frustration, use "Will you...?"**

4. **To say no courteously, use "You can..."**

5. **To save time, give the reason first**

6. **To reduce tension, call anyway**

Technique 1: Use a warm and cooperative tone of voice

Have you ever called someone and had them say all the right words, only to leave you still feeling as though they were irritated with you? If so, there was probably an edge in the person's tone of voice.

With practice, it is possible to remove irritation from your voice. The following exercises will help.

DEEP BREATHING

When you anticipate that your voice or delivery may turn people away and slow you down, lean back and take 60 seconds to breathe deeply. As you relax, breathe in very slowly. Hold your breath for a few seconds. Then breathe out slowly. Repeat for 60 seconds. This is an emergency treatment for your tone of voice.*

VIGOROUS EXERCISE

Carving out time for vigorous exercise also pays off. You not only sound better, you think better and are certainly better to be around. (See Chapter 3, on burnout, for more specific ideas.)

* For more information, see *The Telephone and Time Management* by Dru Scott (Crisp Publications, 1988).

Six Cooperation Techniques (CONTINUED)

Technique 2: To build confidence, use "I will..."

Both you and your customers benefit when you use the "I will..." technique.

Your customers will have even more respect for your competence. Many customers feel annoyed when they hear, "I'll try..." but they calm down when they hear, "I will."

Here is an example: Assume that you are the customer. You are calling to have a new dining table delivered. Imagine how irritated you might feel if you heard, "I will try and have someone there on Thursday, so be sure to be there all day."

A much more effective approach would be: "I will check with our warehouse about scheduling and I will call you back before 12:00 today to let you know the exact time and day we can deliver your new dining table."

Customers like knowing specifically what you will do. Then they are not left in the dark. "I'll try..." is too vague.

When you tell your customers the specific actions you will take, you build their confidence in you. This also helps them understand why you may not have an immediate answer.

You also benefit personally by using the "I will..." technique. When you say, "I will..." and list the steps that you will take, you give yourself a head start. You mentally condition yourself to take the needed action. "I will..." offers advantages for you—and for your customers.

EXERCISE: USING "I WILL..."

Here are samples to get you started:

❖

Rather Than:

1. "I'll try and get an answer for you from Product Coordination."

2. "I'll try and transfer your call to Maintenance. You shouldn't have called me."

3. "Can't you see we're busy? It will take at least half an hour to get that information to you."

4. "I'm sorry you had to call back. You know credit people. Nothing makes them hurry."

5. "Your timing couldn't have been worse. Did you have to call at the end of the day?"

6. "I'll try and get that information for you today, but it may take me longer."

7. "I don't know, but I can try."

8. "I don't know the status of your trouble."

Replace With:

"I will call Product Coordination and I will get back to you before 12:00."

"I will transfer your call to Maintenance. They can answer your question."

"I will get back to you before 4:00."

"I will _____

_____ ."*

"I will _____

_____ ."*

"I will _____

_____ ."*

"I will _____ ."*

"I will _____

_____ ."*

Six Cooperation Techniques (CONTINUED)

Technique 3: To reduce frustration, use "Will you...?"

Use the "Will you...?" technique to help with the following situations:

- Avoid the irritation that people often feel when they hear "You have to..." Those three words make most people bristle. "Will you...?" is a fast and easy way to get what you want.

- Skip the blaming that "You should have..." evokes. A customer is almost automatically going to be defensive when hearing "You should have..." "You made a mistake" also carries the stain of blaming.

- Save the confusion people often feel when they do not know specifically what you want. "It would be good to have the report done by Friday" is not as clear as, "Will you please have the report done by Friday?"

This handy technique smoothes out frustrations. Use "Will you...?" when:

- You need to communicate in a hurry.

- You have not gotten what you wanted in the past. For example, you expected a reply to a question last week, but you did not get it. To avoid repeating that problem you can say, "Will you please have that answer for me before the end of this week?"

If you are not getting what you want and are also tempted to say, "She should know" or "I shouldn't have to tell her," save yourself and your customer time and frustration. The unexpressed expectation hurts everyone. Ask directly with "Will you...?"

❖

Rather Than:	Replace With:
"You have to..."	"Will you...?"
"You should have..."	
"Why didn't you...?"	or
"You made a mistake."	
"I need..."	"Will you please...?"

EXERCISE: USING "WILL YOU...?"

Will you please circle each statement **A** for *agree* or **D** for *disagree*?

1. People respond better to "Will you please complete this job?"   A   D
   than to "You have to get this job done."

2. If you ask, "Will you please?" people will not take you seriously.   A   D

3. If you say, "Will you?" people will think you are so nice that   A   D
   they will be calling you all the time and will keep you from
   getting your work done.

4. Some of the time, "Will you please?" works just as well as "Will   A   D
   you?"

5. "I need the information by Friday" is only a statement, and in   A   D
   response a person may or may not tell you if the information
   will be provided.

6. When you ask directly by saying, "Will you?" you save every-   A   D
   one time because people do not need to guess what you want.

7. The "Will you?" technique will not work as well if you use a   A   D
   sarcastic tone of voice.

See author's responses on page 116.

Six Cooperation Techniques (CONTINUED)

Technique 3: To Reduce Stress, Use "Will You...?"

A quick way to replace language that can offend

The "Will you...?" technique can be used not only to reduce frustration, but also to reduce stress and strained relationships brought on by unfulfilled expectations. Rather than implying blame when expectations are not met, set up the situation for success in the future by asking directly "Will you...?"

Here are some samples to get you started:

❖

Rather Than:	Replace With:
1. "You made a mistake."	"Will you double-check this number for me?"
2. "You should have called earlier."	"Will you call us as soon as you know of any change on the order?"
3. "Why didn't you call us when you found out about the changes?"	"Will you call us as soon as you find out about a change? That lead time is so important.

EXERCISE: USING "WILL YOU...?"

Will you please rewrite the following statements, beginning with "Will you..." to form questions that will reduce stress?

─────────────────────── ❖ ───────────────────────

Rather Than:	Replace With:

1. "You have to fill out these forms."

   "Will you _____

   _____ ?"

2. "I wasn't there when that problem happened. They should have given you the information."

   "Will you _____

   _____

   _____ ?"

3. "You have to call us before Friday."

   "Will you _____

   _____

   _____ ?"

4. "You never give me the data I request."

   "Will you _____

   _____

   _____ ?"

5. "Those two employees are just standing and visiting with each other. They should see how busy I am and help me."

   "Will you _____

   _____

   _____ ?"

Six Cooperation Techniques (CONTINUED)

Technique 4: To say no courteously, use "You can..."

Use the "You can..." technique to achieve the following:

- Gain the appreciation of others when you say no in a courteous way. Imagine how someone might feel being told, "You can't have it today. You have to wait until tomorrow for the material." A much more courteous expression would be, "You can have the material tomorrow." We respond more favorably to hearing what we can do or have.

- Ninety percent of the people will understand that you are saying no, but you may run into someone who still says, "I want it today." In such a case, go to Plan B: "I'm sorry. The material is not ready today. It will be ready tomorrow." You will not need to use Plan B very often. Most people catch on the first time.

- Save time by simultaneously answering the next question most people would otherwise ask, "You said that I can't have it today. Well, when can I have it?"

- Make your job easier. Many people find it difficult to say no and prefer to find some way to be of assistance. The "You can" approach offers this way of being of service.

You will find many opportunities to use this technique in your professional and personal life. Specifically, say "You can..." when:

- You cannot provide exactly what your customer is requesting, but you do have an alternative.

- You want to communicate your sincere interest in service even though you may not be able to be of assistance right now.

- Your customer may not know exactly what he or she is requesting. Giving people an option often stimulates their thinking.

Positive Options for "No"

You can say "no" in a positive way by telling people what you can do. Here are some samples to get you started.

───────────────────────── ❖ ─────────────────────────

Rather Than:	Replace With:
1. "I don't know anything about that. It's not my job. You have to check with Finance."	*"You can get that information from Finance."*
2. "You have to request that item in units of 10. We can't get you a single item."	*"You can request that item in units of 10."*
3. "You can't give us the information over the phone. We can't get it approved until we have it in writing."	*"You can have the order approved when we receive the information in writing."*

EXERCISE: USING "YOU CAN..."

❖

Rather Than:

1. "We don't have that data. You have to call Central Services."

2. "There's nothing I can do. You have to talk with a manager."

3. "That's not our responsibility. You have to get that taken care of by your local organization."

4. "You have to give us two days notice to have that kind of job done."

5. "We won't have the quality of material you want to stock until next week. We only have a lower quality available today."

Replace With:

1. "You can _____
   _____
   _____."

2. "You can _____
   _____
   _____."

3. "You can _____
   _____
   _____."

4. "You can _____
   _____
   _____."

5. "You can _____
   _____
   _____."

Technique 5: To save time, give the reason first

Using the technique of "give the reason first" achieves the following important results:

- The human mind is created with the desire to know why. Think how often a growing child asks, "Why?" When someone is providing information, the question that darts through most listeners' minds and absorbs most of their concentration is "Why?" Capitalize on that reality. Give the reason first.

- You get people's attention more rapidly when you explain the reason first. For example: "To save you money…" or "Here is the answer to your question."

Use the technique of "give the reason first" when:

- You are communicating technical information that the other person may not understand.

- You think the other person may not cooperate.

- The other person may not know you or may not trust your experience.

Use the other person's reason. You get even more cooperation when you express how your message will benefit your customer. Here are some examples:

"To help save you time…"

"To help me complete your request more rapidly…"

"So that I can access you records…"

How to Say "Why" First

People cooperate more readily when you share the purpose first. Here are some samples to get you started.

Rather Than:	Replace With:
1. "You have to use one of our service facilities. It keeps your costs down."	*"To keep your costs down, will you use our service facilities?"*
2. "I can't see if a final adjustment has been issued without your job number."	*"So that I can check and see if your final adjustment has been issued, will you please give me your job number?"*
3. "Why can't you get your processing done on time? I can't call the client with an answer until you give me this information."	*"The client is eager for an answer. Will you please give me this information?"*

EXERCISE: GIVING THE REASON FIRST

❖

Rather Than:

1. "I can't get those summaries completed because your hand-writing is too sloppy. You have to print it so I can read it."

2. "You should have sent the docu-ment. We can't process your renewal without it."

3. "We can't give you a new identification number on the phone. We have to mail it to you. We have to protect your account."

4. "Can't you see I'm busy with a rush project? I can't do your report until this afternoon."

5. "I can't give you a status report right now. I need to isolate the trouble first."

Replace With:

_____

_____

_____

_____

_____

_____

_____

_____

_____

_____

_____

_____

_____

_____

_____

Six Cooperation Techniques (CONTINUED)

Technique 6: To reduce tension, call anyway

The limit of what customers accept if you keep them informed of your progress can be amazing. On the other hand, if you do not let people know what is happening and then surprise them with a delay, there will probably be trouble. When you anticipate and keep people informed about a potential delay, they are much more cooperative.

You also benefit from keeping others informed. Nothing is quite so draining as knowing that you have negative news to tell someone, gritting your teeth when the telephone rings and hoping that person is not on the line. When you call anyway, you take control. You call when you are ready rather than waiting until your customer has erupted into a rage and is calling you.

Call anyway. You reduce your feelings of tension and you build your customer's trust in you.

Use the following discussion questions to sharpen your skill in this problem-preventing approach.

EXERCISE: CALLING ANYWAY

When you have negative news to tell someone, how does this affect your concentration? And how do you feel whenever the telephone rings?

_____

_____

_____

How does it waste your time when you wait and put off calling with negative news?

_____

_____

_____

What are some specific techniques that you can use to get yourself to call anyway?

_____

_____

Why do people appreciate knowing negative news rather than not hearing anything?

_____

_____

_____

CHAPTER 7

—— RECAP OF TECHNIQUES ——

To get the most out of this chapter, check the techniques that you will use more frequently.

I WILL:

- ❑ Use a warm and cooperative tone of voice… **to reduce hostility**

- ❑ Use "I will…" *to build confidence*

- ❑ Use "Will you…" *to reduce frustration*

- ❑ Use "You can…" *to say no courteously*

- ❑ Give the reason first…*to save time*

- ❑ Call anyway…*to reduce stress*

Benefits come with practice. If you are using a technique 75 percent of the time, increase it to 100 percent. Make your job easier by making it easier for others to do what you want. Remember, practice makes permanent.

For Reinforcement Say to Yourself:

"I make it easy for people to cooperate with me.
I find good techniques which can be tailored to fit my personality and the situation.
I have less frustration because I use the techniques at every opportunity."

———————————— ❖ ————————————

Now that you have some specific tools in hand, what overall system will help you use the tools on a continuing basis? The answer is ongoing customer feedback and that is what the next chapter explores.

Building Motivation with Customer Feedback

Enjoy the Benefits of Getting Systematic Feedback

P R E V I E W

The biggest reason that people do not provide quality customer satisfaction is:

They do not have adequate information about when they are and are not satisfying customers.

The cure is feedback.

❖

People Need to Know How They Are Doing

"Hey, hey, hey! We met goal at 3:30 today."

The kind of energy that the above statement conveys will not come through any amount of "attaboys" or "attagirls." Employee benefits will not produce it. Good supervision is not enough. Good people are not enough. Even the techniques for getting cooperation are not enough.

To sustain a high level of motivation, we all need feedback about how well we are achieving our targets.

The Missing Ingredient

Abraham Maslow, the famous psychologist, pointed out that satisfied needs are not motivators. This is true. We are motivated more by what we are missing. Targets give us something to miss. Feedback lets us know how we are doing.

CHECK FOR CUSTOMER SATISFACTION

Give yourself a head start with these personal benefits by checking with your customers for satisfaction. Place a check mark by the objective that is most important to you.

I PLAN TO:

❏ Reduce stress by having a focus that is energizing and motivating.

❏ Save time by avoiding having to do things that my customer does not really want.

❏ Enjoy more satisfaction by learning to skip "How am I doing?" concerns. When you check with customers for satisfaction, you know how you are doing.

Some people might say, *"I know I do good work because I've done it for years."* But they never really know how good their work is until they check with their customers for satisfaction.

You might hear, *"Oh, I know they are satisfied. If they aren't, they always complain."* Again, the provider really does not know whether the customer is satisfied. Some customers will complain to dozens of others without ever telling the organization that provided the product or service.

Another dangerous comment is *"I know what they want."* This approach often causes problems because the customer receives a product or service that is not what was expected.

People Need to Know How They Are Doing (CONTINUED)

WHAT HAS HAPPENED TO YOU?

Think of some situations in your professional or personal life in which you were the customer. Pick one in which the service was not up to your expectations and the person providing the service did not bother checking with you to see how satisfied you were. Write the responses in the spaces provided below.

Situation in which you were the customer and you did not get what you wanted:

_____

_____

_____

_____

_____

How did you feel and what did you do later?

_____

_____

_____

_____

_____

CASE STUDY:
Greg and Customer Feedback

Greg, a carpenter, was overheard to say: "I always knew that we were supposed to do the best job possible, and it never bothered me if I had to go back to the job site two or three times before completing the repair.

"Then our team started getting feedback on the requests that we handled. Our clients were asked, 'Was the job completed on the first visit?' The answer was usually, 'No.'

"My boss had told me to complete everything on the first trip (one trip), but I didn't think it was that important. I only recognized how important it was when our department starting putting 'job completed first visit' on the customer feedback form.

"Although we thought we were doing a good job, our customers reported that they wanted the repair work completed the first trip. Now I call the person making the request before I go. With a list of questions, I find out what tools and materials we need to take. It has made the job easier. And with customer feedback my boss spends less time telling me things."

Customer feedback makes the job easier!

A Simple System for Obtaining Feedback

Asking for feedback will help you get your priorities into focus. But it is not always easy to get feedback from your customers—even from those with whom you work most closely. They may think that you should automatically know how they feel about your service. Or they may dislike giving any negative feedback that "might hurt your feelings." The fear of hurting someone's feelings often ends up wasting time because important information is not communicated, and in the end feelings get hurt anyway.

THREE PLUSES AND THREE MINUSES

Here is a streamlined technique for obtaining valuable feedback.* Tell a customer: "I want to make sure my work is satisfying your expectations. Will you tell me three things you like about my work? And three things we need to do to improve our service?"

By asking for the pluses first, you encourage people to get those valuable minuses on the table where you can deal with them.

People sometimes hesitate asking for feedback because they believe that if they asked, the customer will not stop spilling out complaints and demands. This rarely happens. Most people are pleased to be asked and their comments are moderate and helpful.

* For more information on this, read *You've Got To Be Believed To Be Heard* by Bert Decker (St. Martin Publications, 1992)

Protect Yourself with Ongoing Feedback

Ongoing feedback will build a productive foundation for you. If you depend only on the complaints and compliments that are occasionally volunteered, you are on shaky footing. Why? Because robbed of ongoing feedback, the complaint triples in impact. One complaint can cloud all the good work you have accomplished in previous transactions with a customer. By requesting regular feedback, you will not only earn the respect of your customer, you will also begin to hear positive comments about how your service has improved.

Get Going on Customer Feedback

It is easy to lull yourself into a false security if you do not get ongoing feedback from customers.

- **What are some practical ways by which work groups can get input from the people they serve?**

- **Why is systematic feedback important?**

- **What are some examples of feedback systems that work well?**

The questionnaire on the next page offers some ideas that will help you formulate a systematic feedback mechanism that works for you.

Get Systematic Feedback from Your Customers

Open the Door to More Motivation

To stimulate your thinking, the following survey is one method you might use systematically to gather feedback from the people you serve. As you look at the sample survey statements, think of issues or indicators that will be useful in your own survey. Fill in the name of your own organization in the spaces provided.

Sample Customer Survey

Ask the people you serve: On a scale of 1 to 10, with 10 being the best, how would you rate each of these statements?

1. People at _____ communicate that they want to serve me.

   1   2   3   4   5   6   7   8   9   10

2. The quality of work provided by_____ is excellent.

   1   2   3   4   5   6   7   8   9   10

3. _____ people keep me so well-informed that there are no surprises.

   1   2   3   4   5   6   7   8   9   10

4. _____ meets agreed-upon deadlines.

   1   2   3   4   5   6   7   8   9   10

5. The work we receive from _____ is a good value.

   1   2   3   4   5   6   7   8   9   10

6. I am recommending _____ for future jobs.

   1   2   3   4   5   6   7   8   9   10

Other Comments:

Name (Optional): _____

The Best Kind of Customer Feedback

You save the most time and build the best teamwork when you have feedback that is:

✔ **Ongoing**

✔ **Specific**

✔ **Centered on the end-use customer**

✔ **Focused on a limited number of vital indicators**

✔ **Available on a timely basis**

✔ **Available to all key people in the organization, regardless of level**

✔ **Portrayed on a line graph. When the desired results are achieved, the line goes up.**

Why are these feedback features so important? What problems do they prevent?

_____

_____

CONSIDER YOUR OWN RESPONSIBILITIES

Can you provide the name or job title of five people for whom you provide work or a service? When did you last check with each to see how well you are satisfying his or her expectations?

	NAME	MOST RECENT FEEDBACK DATE
1.	_____	
2.	_____	
3.	_____	
4.	_____	
5.	_____	

TALK ABOUT CUSTOMER FEEDBACK

To get the most value from feedback, follow these three guidelines:

- **Talk successes**
- **Talk specifics**
- **Talk daily**

Since feedback is such an important means of motivation, make some notes in the spaces provided and discuss your comments with your manager.

1. Considering that our work can be oriented toward problem solving, why is it important to talk about successes in customer satisfaction?

   _____

   _____

2. When we receive feedback that our work has satisfied customers, it is easy to ignore it. Why is it so easy to disregard positive feedback?

   _____

   _____

3. An "attaboy" rarely works. It sounds insincere. On the other hand, discussing specifics will communicate real substance. This is particularly important when talking about positive customer feedback. What are some examples of specific, positive customer feedback that you have given or received during the last month?

   _____

   _____

4. Talking about customer feedback each day keeps customer satisfaction in focus. What systems and habits can you use to make sure you talk about customer feedback each day?

   _____

   _____

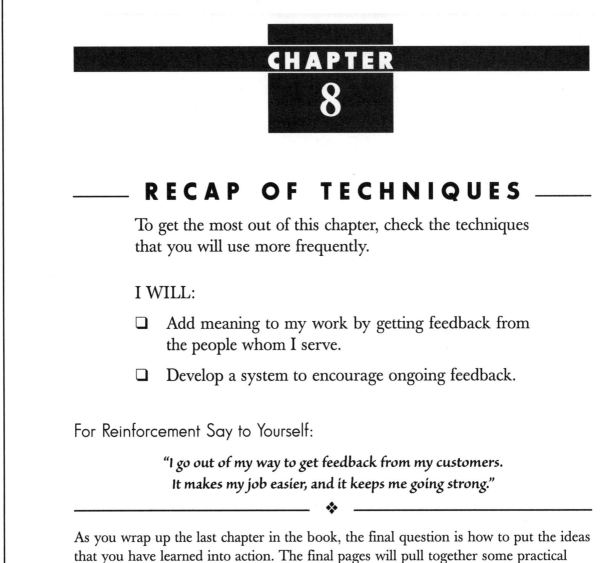

CHAPTER
8

— RECAP OF TECHNIQUES —

To get the most out of this chapter, check the techniques that you will use more frequently.

I WILL:

❏ Add meaning to my work by getting feedback from the people whom I serve.

❏ Develop a system to encourage ongoing feedback.

For Reinforcement Say to Yourself:

*"I go out of my way to get feedback from my customers.
It makes my job easier, and it keeps me going strong."*

❖

As you wrap up the last chapter in the book, the final question is how to put the ideas that you have learned into action. The final pages will pull together some practical ways to reduce stress, get more done and help you build good customer relationships.

CHAPTER

9

How to Keep It Going

*Three Secrets to Help You
Find the Fun in Reinforcement*

— P R E V I E W —

GIVE YOURSELF MORE BLUE RIBBONS.
Reinforce yourself for using good customer relationship skills, building good relationships and earning repeat business.

HAND OUT MORE BLUE RIBBONS.
You are not in this alone. Reinforce the people around you for doing a good job with customers.

TREAT THIS BOOK AS A TOOL KIT.
When you run into something that you want to improve, reach for this tool kit and pick the ideas that will help you handle that customer and build that relationship.

❖

Success Secret 1: Give Yourself More Blue Ribbons

It is an ugly reality. Few people call to thank you for finding a solution. Few e-mails are sent to tell you everything arrived on time. And even fewer customers write to your boss to express appreciation for your good work.

This ugly reality takes its toll. It is easy for people to stop caring about customers. People lose their motivation. They let the telephone ring. And they start saying, "No one appreciates all that I have to do."

If this were a perfect world, this would not happen. But it does happen and that's why the first secret for finding the fun in reinforcement works.

Give yourself more blue ribbons. Do not wait for customers to call or bosses to pat you on the back. Take charge of the situation because it is an important situation. Give yourself more blue ribbons for good work.

This does not necessarily mean going down to the trophy store and buying a bag of actual blue ribbons, but it does mean being able to look at a situation when you have done a job well, pat yourself on the back and figuratively put a blue ribbon on your wall.

You can give yourself a big blue ribbon by going back to the section of Chapter 1, entitled "Writing Your Own Success Story."

It is enormously satisfying not only to do something well but also to know why you did it well.

Give yourself more blue ribbons.

Reinforce yourself for using good customer relationship skills, building good relationships and earning repeat business.

Success Secret 2:
Hand Out More Blue Ribbons

Mention reinforcing others for doing a good job with customers in some groups and you will hear cries of:

- **"Why should I? No one hands me blue ribbons."**

- **"That's not my job."**

- **"I don't have time."**

Yet taking the time to appreciate others for doing a good job is actually selfish, because the centuries-old saying is true: "There is more happiness in giving than in receiving."

Giving recognition to others changes the direction of your energy from inward to outward. Giving recognition to others increases your energy. And it builds a spirit of cooperation which helps everyone. So there are several answers to the question, "Why should I?"

The declaration "That's not my job" bears a closer look. In today's fast-paced, open-structured organizations, recognition is now everybody's job. Particularly if you want to build relationships and get ahead.

The assertion that "I don't have time" does not measure up to the facts. In actuality, if you spend a few minutes writing a quick thank you note to someone, you will receive in return many more minutes of feeling good about doing the right thing.

Hand out more blue ribbons.

*Lift your own spirit. Reinforce the people around you
for doing a good job with customers.*

Success Secret 3:
Treat This Book as a Tool Kit

If the evening is stormy and the fireplace is crackling and you are sitting in a velvet wing chair, chances are you would not want to curl up with a copy of this book. It has a different place.

The place is near your work area. Treat it as a tool kit for which you can reach when you have a special job to do. Keep it handy so that you can reach for it when you run into a situation that you want to improve.

If you are like most people, when you read this book the first time, you will pick two or three ideas that you can use right away.

Then, when you run into new situations, you can reach for the book again, turn the pages and find an idea that fits your situation today.

Treat this book as a tool kit.

When you run into something that you want to improve, reach for this tool kit and pick the ideas that will help you handle that customer and build that relationship.

CASE STUDY
Sarah Shares Her Story

Sarah stood at the front of the conference table, looked at the group of new supervisors and laughed at herself as she shared her story: "When I first became a supervisor, I expected my crew to take everything I said to them, write it on their hearts and use it every day. Well, they didn't. They had too many other things screaming for their attention."

Sarah decided that she needed to provide reinforcement. So she started looking for new ways to reinforce the ideas that she wanted the members of her group to use. She gave them books. She gave them training. And she even started contests to encourage using good ideas.

Sarah went on to share, "Now I smile when someone comes to me and says that so and so won't give her what she wants. Now it's fun to ask her to reach for her copy of *Customer Satisfaction* and open it to the chapter "Getting What You Want.""

Sarah went on to explain how she and her team member would sit down for a couple of minutes with the book open in front of them and scan for an idea that her team member had read and was now ready to use.

CHAPTER 9

─── RECAP OF TECHNIQUES ───

To take away the most from this chapter, look at the following key concepts and check the ones that fit you.

- ❑ Give yourself more blue ribbons.
- ❑ Hand out more blue ribbons.
- ❑ Treat this book as a tool kit.

For Reinforcement Say to Yourself:

*"Using good customer relationship skills saves me time,
helps my professional and personal life and adds to my long-term success."*

❖

Remember the Customer Satisfaction Essentials

For more long-term success, build customer relationships for repeat business opportunities.

It is not only serving customers–
> *it is also satisfying them.*

It is not only filling requests–
> *it is also earning the opportunity for repeat business.*

It is not only transactions–
> *it is building long-term relationships.*

BUILDING CUSTOMER RELATIONSHIPS FOR REPEAT BUSINESS

It is more than a motto. It is a way of relating that helps every area of your life, today and tomorrow.

REMEMBER

Build your own Personal Customer Satisfaction Action Plan by listing the techniques with which you would like to start on page viii, at the beginning of this book.

We would love to hear from you. See our feedback form on page 115. Customer satisfaction is important to us, too!

A STORY

The Third Stonecutter and Customer Relationships

We all have a lot to learn from the story of the visitor who was walking along the cobblestone streets of an old European town when he turned the corner and saw three stonecutters working on a cathedral.

The visitor walked up to the first stonecutter and asked what he was doing.

"Can't you see? I'm just cutting stones," was the answer.

So the visitor walked around the corner and asked the same question of the second stonecutter.

"It's obvious. I'm building a wall," was the reply.

Then the visitor walked around to the other side of the cathedral and asked a third stonecutter, "What are you doing?"

The third stonecutter stood and looked up at the arches, the stained glass windows, the spire reaching skyward, and then he looked directly at the visitor and explained:

"I'm not just cutting stones. I'm building a cathedral."

The lesson of the story is still true today. You can be like the third stonecutter if you always remember:

You are not just handling a customer. You are building a relationship.

Your Feedback Is Important

This book is the result of feedback from hundreds of people in research groups and seminars. To ensure that this book is of continuing value, your feedback is vital. For this reason, please take a moment and note three pluses and three minuses for you in reading this book. You are welcome to use this sheet. Thank you for your ideas.

+ _____

+ _____

+ _____

- _____

- _____

- _____

Please mail to: DRU SCOTT
                      106 Point Lobos, Third Floor
                      San Francisco, CA 94121

Author's Suggested Responses

Chapter 4 (Page 43)
"But I Don't Have Customers" Exercise
1-D; 2-A; 3-D; 4-D; 5-D; 6-D; 7-D; 8-A; 9-A

Chapter 5 (Page 55)
"Aim for Satisfaction" Exercise
1-A; 2-D; 3-D; 4-A; 5-A; 6-A; 7-A; 8-A; 9-A

Chapter 6 (Page 60)
"Beliefs as a Barrier to Problem Solving" Exercise
1-D; 2-D; 3-D; 4-D; 5-D; 6-A; 7-D; 8-D; 9-A; 10-D

Chapter 7 (Page 83)
Using "Will you...?" Exercise
1-A; 2-D; 3-D; 4-A; 5-A; 6-A; 7-A

Review

CUSTOMER SATISFACTION

**Practical Tools for Employees
of Santa Clara County**

The objectives of the book are:

- to provide techniques for overcoming barriers to customer satisfaction

- to explain why satisfying customers is as important as doing a job

- to show how to use the tools of customer satisfaction

Review Questions for
Customer Satisfaction

Select the best response.

1. If you have not had any complaints, your customers

    A. are probably satisfied.
    B. are probably not satisfied.
    C. may not be satisfied.

2. The secret to resolving most "people problems" is to take things

    A. personally.
    B. professionally.

3. If you ask, "How can we solve this situation," you are

    A. being professional by focusing on the issue.
    B. taking the situation personally by focusing on yourself.
    C. trying to distract the customer from the issue.

4. If your interest in what is happening in the world around you has declined,

    A. you should change your job.
    B. you may be suffering from burnout.
    C. your family life may be suffering.
    D. you should change your lifestyle.

5. When an employee achieves a measurable target,

    A. the employee gains a sense of accomplishment.
    B. the employee will easily grow bored and lose interest.
    C. the employee feels like he or she is making a contribution.
    D. A and C

6. Which of the following does not demonstrate that an employee is taking care of his own needs?

    A. speaking up and putting his ideas in writing
    B. hoping people will recognize his work accomplishments
    C. asking directly what he wants

7. Which of the following are symptoms that you may be suffering from burnout?

   A. complaining
   B. use of artificial stimulants
   C. decreased concentration
   D. impatience
   E. all of the above

8. Taking the time to listen to an upset customer will help you

   A. understand what the customer is thinking.
   B. understand what the customer is feeling.
   C. collect your thoughts.
   D. all of the above

9. Cooperation is more likely to happen if you treat a person with whom you work with

   A. as another employee.
   B. informally.
   C. formally.
   D. as a customer.

10. If an employee knows that she excels at her job simply because she has done it for years,

    A. she still may have weaknesses without quality feedback from customers.
    B. she is correct regardless of customer feedback.
    C. she probably makes mistakes often.
    D. all of the above

11. Customer satisfaction is defined by

    A. the supplier.
    B. the customer.
    C. upper management.

12. Usually, the best procedure in setting a business target is to have

    A. management, employees, and customer set the target.
    B. management set the target.
    C. management and employees set the target.
    D. an analysis of the goals of the competition.

13. When establishing customer targets the employee should

    A. guess what the customer may need without the customer's input.
    B. define the customer's goals without involving the customer.
    C. help the customer define her expectations.

14. It doesn't matter if the customer is right or wrong.

    A. True
    B. False

15. If you believe the customer is wrong, you should

    A. accept the blame anyway.
    B. point out the customer's error.
    C. solve the problem without blaming yourself or others.
    D. avoid dealing with that particular customer.

16. Using blaming statements when something goes wrong

    A. will make you look better to the customer.
    B. wastes time and is unproductive.
    C. will help get the problem resolved.

17. When you encounter a difficult person,

    A. keep the spotlight away from yourself.
    B. focus on the issue at hand.
    C. both of the above

18. Which is the better course of action when telling a customer a repair has been delayed?

    A. Do not call the customer until the work is completed.
    B. Tell the customer, "In order to fix the problem properly, we had to order a new part, therefore…"
    C. Tell the customer, "Your repair is going to take longer than expected, because…"

19. When you tell your customers the actions you will take by using an "I will…" statement,

    A. it builds their confidence in you.
    B. they'll understand why you may not have an immediate answer.
    C. you mentally condition yourself to take action.
    D. all of the above

20. You should call a customer even if that person is irate

    A.   rather than waiting until your customer is calling you.
    B.   because this reduces your own tension and builds your customer's trust in you.
    C.   because informed customers are much more cooperative.
    D.   all of the above

21. Customer satisfaction skills improve relationships with

    A.   family and friends.
    B.   people inside the organization.
    C.   people outside the organization.
    D.   all of the above

22. Treating your boss as a customer

    A.   will save you time.
    B.   is a waste of your customer satisfaction skills.
    C.   will undermine the respect your boss has for you.

23. Waiting for complaints and compliments will make your job more pleasant than asking for ongoing customer feedback.

    A.   True
    B.   False

24. Once you understand the skills which help increase customer satisfaction,

    A.   you no longer need to work on them.
    B.   your old habits will no longer affect you.
    C.   you must practice these skills to reap the benefits.

25. Two effective methods to verify customers' expectations are to begin your sentence "I know..." or "I understand..."

    A.   True
    B.   False

Qualitative Objectives for *Customer Satisfaction*

To explain why satisfying customers is as important as doing a job

Questions 1, 9, 11, 12, 16, 21, 22, 23

To show how to use the tools of customer satisfaction

Questions 2, 3, 5, 6, 7, 8, 13, 15, 17, 18, 19, 20

To explain the benefits of maintaining customer satisfaction

Questions 4, 10, 14, 24, 25

Answer Key

1. C (97)	6. B (27)	11. B (47)	16. B (59)	21. D (10)
2. B (15)	7. E (24)	12. A (52)	17. C (18-19)	22. A (41-42)
3. A (19)	8. D (67)	13. C (52)	18. B (90)	23. B (100-101)
4. B (23)	9. D (37)	14. A (58)	19. D (80)	24. C (94)
5. D (28)	10. A (97)	15. C (59)	20. D (92)	25. B (70)

Please complete the following to obtain your certificate of completion for this course:

Completed forms should be submitted to:

> Employee Development
> Santa Clara County Government Center
> 70 West Hedding
> Lower Level West Wing
> San Jose, CA 95110
> Tel: 408-299-2186
> Fax: 408-280-5722

Level I

Tell us what you liked about this course?

_____

_____

_____

What could we do better?

_____

_____

_____

Are there any others topics you might like to see covered in future classes at Santa Clara County?

_____

_____

_____

Level II

Please fill in the number of correct answers from the assessment on the previous pages [   ]

Your name and Pony address: Date: _____

_____

_____

_____